Praise

I like the way Rohadi thinks. I like the way Rohadi's heart beats. I like the way Rohadi leans into healthy scepticism without the caustic critique of the cynic. I love it when people have the integrity and courage to allow the Spirit to lead them into becoming the answer to their own prayers. Rohadi has done so, not just by penning this great little book, but by living it out, day by day. Let us do the same.

- David Ruis
National Director of Vineyard Canada

For many years, Rohadi has been a voice calling out from edges of the church in Canada. This book is a helpful primer for people that want to join him by intentionally choosing to live out the gospel at the edges of Christendom. His perspectives are raw and real. You owe it to yourself to take a look.

- Jared Siebert
National Director of Church Planting,
Free Methodist Church in Canada

Rohadi wrestles with the questions of how we need to re-imagine how we be and do church and mission to engage the "nones" and the "dones" in our Western culture. What deepens his credibility, and gives his message weight, is that Rohadi is a practitioner. I highly commend his thought provoking, prophetic, and hopeful book for practitioners who know in their gut that we need to follow Jesus to the margins where His Kingdom is breaking in!

- Tim Schultz
Director of Mosaic Ministries

Thrive.

Ideas to Lead the Church in post-Christendom.

By: Rohadi

RoBarry Publications, Calgary

Thrive. Ideas to Lead the Church in Post-Christendom.
Copyright © 2018 by Rohadi Nagassar.

Published by RoBarry Publications
PO Box 34252 Westbrook PO
Calgary, Alberta T3C3W2
www.robarry.com

First Edition

ISBN 978-0-9950376-2-5

Book design by V4Victory

Author photo courtesy of Erik McRitchie Photography.

10 9 8 7 6 5 4 3 2 1

SPECIAL SALES
Special quantity discounts available when purchased in bulk by organizations, churches, and special-interest groups. For more information, please email publications@robarry.com.

To: The dreamers, schemers, and idea makers.

Contents

Part IV.
Tests & Enemies

Part V.
Failure & Reward

Foreword

"

Behold, I am doing a new thing;
now it springs forth, do you not perceive it?
I will make a way in the wilderness
and rivers in the desert.

- The Prophet Isaiah

*I*f there is one thing that is constant in the world in which we live, it is change. The magnitude of change is mammoth. The speed of change is accelerating. While the character of Jesus remains the same, incarnational ministry is not the same yesterday, today and forever. For as the well-regarded missiologist David Bosch has said, "if we take the incarnation seriously, the Word has to become flesh in every new context."

But we too easily get settled into the rhythms of life that keep us comfortable, safe and resistant to change. We develop theological arguments to protect our way of life. Like Peter in the book of Acts, we have become comfortable with clear definitions of what food is clean, and what food is unclean. We don't want anyone to tell us any different, even if it happens to be the voice of God. We prefer order to chaos. We like to have everything in its proper place. We don't like to disrupt the status quo, especially if we are benefiting. Things are perfectly fine as they are.

But when God is on the move, he disturbs the comfortable and comforts the disturbed. We see this with Peter and Cornelius, and throughout the book of Acts. The Spirit is blowing wind into the sails of the early church, taking her into uncharted territory, flipping people's understanding, for the sake of those who live apart from God.

God is on the move today. He is giving young people visions, and old people dreams. He is sending prophets to lift our heads out of the sand so that we might behold the current reality of the church, and respond in faith, hope and love. God is sending prophets with apostolic vision to help us realize that there is something greater than our comfort and more important than our security. There is life. There is adventure. There are dreams to be realized.

In *Thrive*, Rohadi not only wakes us up to reality, but he prophetically inspires. His passion for God and people bleed through these pages. His apostolic vision for the church is captivating. He shares hard won nuggets of truth along with his struggles and failures. He's real. He is like the men from the tribe of Issachar, he understands the times in which we live, and what we must do. With theological depth and practical wisdom, Rohadi calls the church to shift from *survive* mode to *thrive* mode.

Like most prophets, he diagnosis the problem poetically, identifying Goldilocks churches and exposing ministry pornography, where leaders seek to clone megachurch pastors, instead of aspiring to create contextually vibrant churches. After diagnosing the problem, he goes to the root of the solution, which is found in a missionary God, a robust gospel and a sent people.

But he doesn't leave us on shore with a boat and no paddles. He invites us to set sail for the open seas, allowing the wind of the Spirit to be our guide into uncharted waters. Rohadi, like the Apostle Paul, takes a hopeful and constructive approach to being the church. He recognizes that church is not a service we go to- it is a state of being. It is being meaningfully connected to God, His people, and mission day by day with all of our life. Church gatherings are good and help orient us to be the church, but going to a church service is no substitute to being the church.

Rohadi calls us to go out to the highways and byways, to go out to the *nones* and the *dones*, if we want to participate in the unfolding kingdom of God. He recognizes that every human being longs for justice, love and beauty, but many have been turned off by the church, or should I say, our current forms of church.

Recently, I met someone through a social app that helps people who live in the same geographical area network around vocational ideas and needs. The young man I shared a meal with had a Jewish upbringing and was "happily" divorced. After discovering that I train church planters in North America, he asked me about my conversion, my life and about Jesus. He was hungry for truth. He was thirsty for reality. He wants to meet up again soon. There are many like him, who will never set foot in a church service, but have genuine interest in Christ. This is why we need to bring the church to them.

Rohadi recognizes that discipleship will either make or break our God-given dreams. He understands that discipleship must move from the margins to the center of our mission. He also recognizes that discipleship is not primarily cerebral. True discipleship requires instruction, but must move to helping people immerse into mission through living examples. If we hope to make missional disciples who live in the world for the sake of the world in the way of Christ, we must disciple people to build communities on mission. Dan White Jr. and I talk about this extensively in our book *The Church as Movement*. For the church to move forward in mission, and for discipleship to be holistic, we must structurally connect discipleship to building communities on mission.

As you read through *Thrive*, you will pick up much proverbial wisdom in how to be an ecclesial architect. One piece that caught my attention was the SpiderFish metaphor. The established church (spider) needs new innovative and experimental churches (starfish) and experimental churches need established churches. Rohadi does a great job describing the strengths and weaknesses of each. This idea of the starfish and spider working together is not just theoretical for me. As the national director for the V3 Church planting movement, we are living into this reality. We would not have been able to train, encourage and support over 150 church planters across

North America in the last five years without the help of an association of churches who generously support our apostolic work.

Thrive is not only an inspirational read with much proverbial wisdom, it also speaks to the enemies and challenges we will face as we embark on this journey. My current PhD studies explore how a theology of the principalities and powers shape a leader's approach to power and mission. One of my dialogue partners is William Stringfellow, who articulates the powers in our current vernacular as *image, ideology* and *institution*. Rohadi does well to warn us that ideology is one of the current idols of our day. I agree that the church must resist liberalism, conservatism, and nationalism, for ideology is idolatry and only leads to death and dehumanization. Any so-called doctrine that keeps us from welcoming all who are made in God's image is demonic and damages our witness. We must remember that the incarnate One through His death, broke the power of him who holds the power of death (Heb. 2:14), so we need not be held captive to the powers, we can live free in obedience.

In the final section of the book, Rohadi reminds us that all entrepreneurs fail, but this should not discourage us, for failure is always at the cutting edge of fruitfulness. The fruit is at the end of the branch, so we must be risk takers, living by faith so that we might please the One who has sent us to be a blessing to all nations. You and I are in a "Kodak moment" of opportunity. If you want to move from complacency to living the dream and vision that God has put in you, then pick up this book and read. Rohadi delivers.

- JR Woodward
Seattle, Washington
Easter Season 2018

Thrive

Daydreams

*W*hat would you do if you won $60 million dollars in the lottery? This isn't the first time you've daydreamed about winning is it? Like many times before, you just saw yourself in a new car, bigger house, on a beach, and paying off debt. Too bad it's only a dream—or is it?

Revealed in your spending spree plans is a small yet critical capability: *you can dream for a better world....* Nobody's lottery dream pictures a life worse off. Rather, you think of the best world money can buy. It starts with selfish indulgences, but when given a chance, eventually you start to think about restoring broken pieces in your world too. Like repairing a playground, funding a new arts program, helping someone through a hard time, providing for your kids, or giving to your favorite charity.

Admittedly, dreaming for a better world is easy to do with $60 million so let's eliminate the sure thing—you're never going to win the lottery. Remove the free money and all that's left is the dream for better. Let's also be more specific with the kind of dream I'm referring to. I'm not talking about a dream like the American Dream of prosperity and success. I'm also not talking about a self-centered dream for community that fits our selfish desires. Dietrich Bonhoeffer warned about such "wishful dreaming" as something God

hates.[1] We don't want to impose our picture for better on community, rather we want to recognize what God is *already* doing in and
beyond community. The dream I'm talking about involves discovering the fullness of God's calling in your life. A dream rooted in
our embodiment to love one another. A dream that emerges when
people around you discover the fullness of God's kingdom that
unfolds in our churches, neighborhoods, and cities. Whether you
can see it or not, *merely holding this kind of dream for better qualifies you as
a primary agent to turn these dreams into reality.* The question is, what's
stopping you? Turns out making dreams and ideas come to life is
hard. That's where this book comes in.

Contained herein is a collection of ideas designed to compel
leaders, mavericks, movers, shakers, church planters, innovators,
pioneers, entrepreneurs, apostles, prophets, pastors, teachers, evangelists, and dreamers of any denomination and creed to live out
their dreams for better in an action of monumental transformation.
Sound exciting? It is! What's not exciting is the current state of the
church.

Here's the problem: *Christianity in the West is in trouble.* Church attendance and membership have dropped, buildings sit empty, tithes
and resources are drying up. I'm not suggesting we'll wake up tomorrow and all the churches will be gone. I am suggesting that the
once powerful and privileged place the church had in our culture
is almost gone. The numbers say Christianity's reach is declining as
a whole in the West. One reason why? As churches lose their own
people, they're not being replaced. Another reason? Society has
pushed the church from the center to the margins. This new reality

---

[1] Dietrich Bonhoeffer, Life Together and Prayerbook of the Bible, vol. 5 of Dietrich Bonhoeffer
Works, ed. Wayne Whitson Floyd Jr. (Minneapolis: Fortress Press, 1996), 36.

leaves church leaders struggling to find answers to stop the exodus. The troubling part is, despite the attempts, few answers seem to be working. The majority of ideas addressing decline are derived from a church opertaing in Christendom, a time when it enjoyed being the center of cultural attention. Proposed answers rely on a return to that privilege rather than figuring out ways to co-create in a new post-Christian culture. This posture explains why churches trying to grow focus most of their resources on improving the service or targeted programming in an attempt to attract people *into* the church's world. The church is accustomed to operating at the center of cultural attention and has yet to discover enough ways to survive outside of it. We must learn how to thrive outside of our past prestige.

Is your community declining? Is it struggling to grow? If it does grow is it mostly because Christians are switching from different churches? Is your church full of people who all look the same? Make about the same salary? Share the same political or theological beliefs? It seems Western Christianity struggles with the problem of sameness. It occurs when Christians fail to live out their calling to be *sent ones,* and instead fall into a rhythm of producing exclusive communities. These communities struggle to bear competent witness to anybody who doesn't look like them or share in the same social network. A culture of sameness contributes to church decline as we embrace security at the cost of losing an identity of love for one another *and the other.* Why do we continue to accept this predominant trend? My aim is to address these deficiencies by building new competencies.

Despite daunting challenges, hope abounds. I believe we live in a moment of great *opportunity,* and a fresh outlook, coupled with God's revolutionary hope, can build a church that thrives in a post-

Christian world. This is where your dreams and ideas for better come into play.[2] You may not believe your ideas qualify, that they're too small and insignificant, but consider this: you've already passed half the test. Half of answering a call is simply holding a picture for better in your world. You demonstrated that when you daydreamed about the imaginary lottery winnings. The other half? Anybody can daydream, but turning dreams into reality is the other half, and it's harder than it looks. Nonetheless, the church is in desperate need of more dreamers answering their call to join God's unfolding kingdom. We need to release and build up new ideas to discover what works and what won't in a new cultural reality. I'm not suggesting we can fix the whole church, nor am I suggesting you can fix your own by yourself. We know Jesus leads the church; however, you are the church, and you are called to participate in God's unfolding hope for your city and beyond.

Still not convinced you hold a critical role in this moment? Picture your hero, perhaps someone you admire or a historical figure. What would the world look like if they never answered the call or lived out their picture for better? They wouldn't be heroes. They would be a nobody—or rather, just like everybody else. What if Mother Teresa thought caring for the poor was a monthly outreach event? What if Gandhi elected to plod his way through the law firm to make partner? Where would we be if Martin Luther King Jr. listened to criticism and became a moderate? None of this happened because these heroes saw wrongs, had a dream for better, and worked to turn their dream real by righting the scales. A vision of better stirred them to face monumental challenges, and as a result, unexpected goodness prevailed. Their work to confront

---

[2] I will use the words "dreams" and "ideas" interchangeably throughout this book.

and change routine ordinary compelled them forward to become extraordinary. What about you?

You might say, "Mother Teresa was extraordinary, but not I. I don't have her courage, passion, humility, patience, _____." Maybe you're right, but don't overlook this important detail: heroines are rarely measured by their grand ideas in the moment. It can take a lifetime before better emerges. During the day, few could grasp the picture Mother Teresa, or Martin Luther King Jr., or Gandhi could see for tomorrow. Eventually, in the end their dream for better became apparent to others, but before these heroes were lauded for their success, they were people who merely yet profoundly said "yes" to make their ideas for better real. They said "yes" to live out a deeply ingrained hope that you and I share: the pursuit to realize our full potential in God's ultimate dream of prevailing goodness.

You may also say, "But there's nothing wrong with being ordinary," and you're right. Ordinary is beautiful and powerful. It's an anecdote to our culture of busy where value is measured in success and public grandeur. Yet, I'm not dismissing an ordinary life. I'm looking to dispose of an ordinary world where settling for decay replaces life.

Somewhere inside each of us is a desire to matter in our own stories. We all want to be valued and discover our full identity. We want to have impact in the things we're good at and make a difference in our lives and the lives of others. But would we call ourselves extraordinary in our own story? Would we call ourselves extraordinary in God's hope? As image bearers of the Creator, we have a built-in longing to live out the full potential of our humanity. What's one way to start? By living out our potential by turning the dreams and ideas God's put in front of us real. In fact, this is the *answer* to how we can lead a church to thrive in post-Christendom.

The thriving church needs to *unlock the potential of the people.* The gifts, the callings, the ideas that stretch beyond the limits of this world and into God's ultimate dream of restoration for the entirety of creation. Your question is this: will you say "yes" to a role to love those around you and live out your picture for better in your neighborhood, city, and beyond? Will you say "yes!" and take the necessary risk to turn your dreams real and make your world a better place?

Chapter 1

Yes to Adventure

"So this, I believe, is the central question upon which all creative living hinges: Do you have the courage to bring forth the treasures that are hidden within you?"
- Elizabeth Gilbert

I loved reading as a kid. When I discovered "choose your own adventure" books I was hooked. I chose the direction for the hero, a device that served to pull me deeper into the written adventure. But as a fail safe, when I entered the dragon's lair on page 78, I made sure to keep my finger on page 42 in case a hasty retreat was necessary. If I selected the right path at each twist and turn it would lead to the eventual happy ending, and we all love happy endings.

One of the reasons why countries in post-colonial Africa struggle to emerge from their poverty is lack of security. People need assurance of basic safety before they can devote attention to issues of development. In North America, there's a greater chance your socio-economic sphere lends to greater security. But with security comes a different kind of hazard. The allure of safety is bred in a culture and economy built on the false premise of scarcity rather than abundance. We think we don't have enough so we strive to accumulate. Society winds up racing towards security in jobs, health, future, and in relationships. On one end of the spectrum security is a fundamental human right for all. On the opposite end, security can breed complacency. Complacent may be a good word to describe the state of many churches today.

Picture the church as a participant in an unfolding adventure story. But unlike choose your own adventure books, we already know the end. The heart of the Christian hope rests in God's story of ultimate rescue and redemption, of all wrongs finally turned right, of heaven and earth restored together forever. It is a triumphant journey where in the end *love wins*. We share the greatest story the world has known but in our cities and towns fewer and fewer people have heard of it. How did this happen? The church has lost its ability to live out its mission. It has become complacent. It's stuck in a mode assuming the world will come to it to find the answers to life's questions. In reality it has lost the capability to tell and live God's love story in a way those outside of church culture can understand and experience. How the church functioned and postured over the past centuries doesn't work to connect in our new and different world. To some this problem is obvious. But others remain ignorant of the facts—Christianity is on the margins of society and it's *not coming back to the center*. Working to reclaim a past life is impossible; what we need are steps to live out faithfully in a new context. If God remains unchanged but the church is disintegrating, it's us—the church—that must change. Despite lost prestige, God's hope remains, and it's for this reason we need new ideas, along with capable storytellers, to live out the fullness of their callings. Your dreams and ideas are important components to turn the tide of decline as we make our small part of the world better. We need brave men and women to take the first, second, and twentieth step outside of their comfort zone to become infused by the character of Jesus and God's dream for our world—the restoration of all things.

Upcoming

This book is designed to help you and your church survive and
thrive in a post-Christian world. It propels you beyond a comfort
and complacency, and into the extraordinary plan God has in store.
It is a guide to help turn the necessary components—your dreams
and ideas for better—real. Five main parts are ahead of you, each
with multiple chapters. Part One will diagnose the problem the
church finds itself in today. I explain the current state of the church,
how we got here, and examine the cultural shifts that have rendered
the contemporary church facing obsolescence. After that we dive
straight into what can be done about decline. We can't do much to
change culture around us, but we can change and respond to our
root callings.

Discovering and embodying our callings as church and Christians is necessary to build the foundation required to thrive in
post-Christendom. Part Two revives an ancient outlook on God's
mission and the church's response. A re-orientation to mission is
required. Along with mission will include our individual role in
community—the witness we bear as Jesus followers.

When we establish a foundation, coupled with a new understanding on how we got to a place of disintegration, we can start
exploring ways forward. Anybody can declare the emperor has no
clothes, but it's quite another to offer solutions. Part Three will
start to interact with your dreams and ideas, while articulating
some building blocks to tip those dreams into action. We will look
at potential solutions that your church can try to survive and thrive
in a post-Christian culture. It may be helpful as you encounter new
ideas in this book to process them through this question (you may

want to earmark this page so you can find it quickly):

> *What is the one act, the one moment, the one choice*
> *you can make to live out your dream for better within*
> *the fullness of God's calling?*

Like any good adventure, eventually you encounter problems. Part Four will talk about the tests and enemies that derail new ideas and inhibit us from moving forward. Spiritual, mental, and social tests will challenge you and your dream for better. Some tests will expose long held beliefs, others the comforts of your known world. I will include warnings about enemies in your wake: people who want to criticize you and your efforts, and one of the greatest enemies of all, yourself. Do you have what it takes to face adversity and die to your own presuppositions in order to prevail? It's the price you have to pay to see that dream and vision unfold. Part Five will conclude our journey on a high note. Rather than the doom and gloom, we consider what a reward in post-Christendom looks like.

The stakes are high, and doing nothing isn't an option. If we fail to respond to our dreams and ideas for better it could spell death of our communities. This worst case scenario can be prevented if we succeed in joining God's hope to love deeply and be radically different for the right reasons.

Embark now on an adventure to take your ideas for better, found within God's dream of restoration, to live them out in your church, neighborhood, city, and beyond. Receive now the call to lurch out of complacent unawareness to discover your role in God's ultimate story: the final triumph of good over evil. Let's begin the journey to turn ideas for better real.

A liturgy for turning dreams real.

Oh Lord, pour out your Spirit on all people.
Grant your sons and daughters stories to live,
Your old men and women dreams of grandeur,
Your young men and women visions of better.

Part I.

Disintergration, Denial, Dysfunction

"Where we discover the magnitude of the problem."

Chapter 2

Our Ordinary World

"Vulnerability is the birthplace of innovation, creativity and change."
- Brene Brown

*E*pic journeys begin by introducing potential heroes living in their mundane ordinary world. Think of the hobbits from J.R.R. Tolkien's books. The Shire boasted a simple agrarian existence complete with six meals a day. The hobbits were unconcerned about the world beyond their borders, never considering the prospect of adventure because their grass was green enough. Their complacency, however, had a drawback. They were oblivious to the growing danger that lurked in Middle Earth; one that threatened their very existence. They were in denial evil could ever reach them, and were happy to stay ignorant to the shifting world.

Many churches are acting like the hobbits of the Shire. In denial, and perhaps even ignorant, to the extent cultural shifts in North America are rendering traditions irrelevant. Aggressive opposition to the loss of cultural privilege, ignoring culture shifts beyond the church walls, or facilitating small yet inconsequential changes are just a few ways churches have responded. Those that appear to be surviving rely on sub-cultures where Christians only associate with other Christians. It's an exclusivity that produces Christians who are oblivious, unconcerned, and/or disconnected from the world outside of the church walls. We spend a lot of time creating substitute worlds because protecting what we're familiar with is safe. But is it good for us?

Some Christians take compartmentalizing further by defining their own "sacred" and rejecting what they deem "profane". The process of protecting belief systems often means becoming antagonistic to mainstream culture, despising what differs from set doctrinal lists of morals, rules, and religious regulations. But is it worth the effort? Have these approaches propelled the church forward into resilience and growth? Or does it represent the final gasp for a body in death throes? Protecting familiarity is like building a metaphorical ark, full of our belief systems, to weather shifting cultures. But in the process of building closed communities we unknowingly (or perhaps knowingly) ignore the magnitude of God's mission. A mission we're invited to participate in, and one that is already working to restore our neighborhoods, cities, and beyond.

Gold Standard

Christena Cleveland, in her book, *Disunity in Christ,* describes a perception called the *gold standard effect.* It describes the exaggeration of manufactured differences between groups of people. If a church surrounds itself with people who think, look, act, and believe the same things, they will create an alternative universe where the internal beliefs, ideologies, and goals are "normal." But it goes further than that. The "normal" becomes the standard for what's normal for all other outsider groups, including other churches that don't look the same.[3] The assumed "normal" blinds us to the value only

---

[3] Cleveland, *Disunity in Christ,* 70.

discovered in differences (the beauty in diversity found in the body of Christ for example), and serves to makes outsiders invisible.

It's not easy to accept change, but without it the ways the church can reverse unmitigated decline drops. We need many ways to help us see the world through a different set of eyes. We need sight to discover that what lies beyond our own familiarity and comforts is a new journey God has already set before us.

The Average Sunday Church

Jon was a pastor of an average church, of an average size, in an average city. This particular Sunday was no different than any other. The music was on point, the service started on time, and the seats were just as full as the previous week. As he stepped to the pulpit, ready to start the annual series on mission, he couldn't help but notice how everything looked...the same. It wasn't a question about ethnicity, although there was little variety. It was something deeper. He thought about the small groups, which were not growing but certainly not shrinking. The outreach and Sunday school ministries had faithful volunteers. No, it was something to do with the service, not this particular one, but in general. It finally struck him: there was rarely a new face at service. On a whim, Jon thought of an impromptu exercise for the congregation.

"Good morning everyone, if you would humor me for a moment. To launch our missions series I would like to start with some ad-hoc research. Could everyone please stand? I'm going to share a few scenarios, and once you hear one that fits you, please sit down. Ready?"

Jon looked across the standing congregation and began.

"How many of you can't remember a time when you haven't known God? As far back as your memory goes you've always been a Christian." Over half of the congregation sits.

"Now, how many of you came to faith as a kid?" About two-thirds of those left standing sit.

"How many of you became Christians as teenagers?" A few more individuals sit, leaving a choice few standing, the outliers of the community.

Jon's hunch was confirmed. The congregation was full of lifelong Christians. Jon realized that his series on missions wasn't going to address the deeper issue that was lingering longer than he'd care to admit. All the discipleship classes, outreach events, and leadership development had yet to address the disconnect in Jon's church between people inside and people outside the church building walls. What was even more disappointing, they all seemed content with the current arrangement.

Did you follow along Jon's questions picturing your own community? Are your results similar? The church has struggled for years, perhaps decades, to connect with the world outside of its walls. It's a primary reason why churches, big or small, have very few adults come to faith. The odd lapsed Christian coming back perhaps, but it's rare when an adult with no prior faith exposure has a conversion experience. The church can't seem to connect with outsiders who don't already fit into existing Christian culture. Jon's church reveals our struggle to live out the Christian character of loving the other. The "others" are the people who don't look like the average demographic in your church. The neighbors who live outside of the church's ingrained culture, and would struggle to belong if they ever visited. To what extent has the church accepted this prevailing trend as normative? To dig deeper, what's at stake for Jon's church, and all the other churches like his, if they don't figure out ways to connect with people outside of the community?

Today, the growing minority of people in our cities have little connection to church culture. They are people who ask questions like, "Why is there a person hanging from the plus sign (+) around your neck?" (pointing to a crucifix on a gold chain). Or those who need clarification for words like "sin" or "atonement." We must concede to a reality that this demographic will soon become a majority and right now the church doesn't know what to do.

Chapter 3

Nones & Dones

The times they are a-changing.
- Bob Dylan

*M*y grandma used to spend Sunday mornings attending a church service down the road from her home. A few decades ago, the majority of her community attended one of the three churches in the neighborhood. Grandma and her church represented an era in which most people went to church or at least knew the church stories. The same can't be said today. Something has changed.

The next time you take a drive through the heart of the city, look out for the old churches. Metropolitan cities are full of old church buildings (usually mainline denominations) in prime locations. Despite the ornate steeples, stained glass windows, and tiered balconies within, something seems out of place. If you were to visit a weekly service chances are those balconies would sit empty. Today, these once prominent buildings sit as an eerie reminder of a bygone era of church prestige. Something has changed.

I was reminded of this era driving through the Canadian province of Nova Scotia. White steeple after white steeple dotted the neighborhoods. I was particularly fascinated with their names: the "First Church" of every stripe, color, and denomination. Many I had never heard of before. It was also a month before Christmas, so every church sign casually noted how their church pageant would be different from that church down the road. These churches were living in a world where competition between churches was normal, and denominational affiliation, along with special service features, were differentiating factors.

Today, churches are shrinking but competition remains, albeit over a market of lifelong Christians. The remaining faithful are less concerned about denominational statements than about pragmatics: what programs are available for kids, youth, families, and how good the preaching is. The church responds by catering to a stagnant supply of Christians who demand its services. In this relationship, the church clings to Christendom, a time of privilege that kept it at the center of cultural attention. Christendom offered the church inherited influence over policies, politics, even economies, all the way down to the day-to-day lives of people. It could wait for the world to come to it. The church in Christendom made little effort to reach beyond because they didn't have to. This passivity contributed to a crippling halt in key church functions like evangelism, outreach, and discipleship.

Who's Church?

It's important to pause and add some context to the term "the church" when it's used in this book. I'm using the term broadly as the holy communion of the saints, albeit localized in the West. In Christendom, I believe churches from all traditions suffer from the "loss" of being pushed to the margins. However, not all churches experience the loss of cultural influence in the same way. Only the church that had power to begin with can lose it. In the West, the benefactors of Christendom are white churches of every tradition ranging from mainline to evangelical, Protestant to Catholic, and liberal to conservative. In America, the bulk of power is held by white Protestant churches (evangelicals). In Canada, white Protestant (mainline) and white Catholic churches held privilege depending on region.

A number of factors contributed to the inheritance of cultural power including the evils of colonialism and slavery. White Christians also dominated culture by sheer numbers. Early settlers across North America were overwhelmingly European and brought with them values and cultures that have remained dominant until recently. For the church, the high water mark for the Christendom era occurred in the 1950s when weekly service attendance hit just under 60% for all Americans (just under 70% in Canada during the same time period).[4] Today the balance has shifted significantly due to two primary reasons.

First, immigration patterns have changed. White Christians are no longer the majority in the American religious landscape (in 2016 they comprised around 41%).[5] Immigration is a primary reason why the Roman Catholic church is one of the few traditions that continues to grow. Second, beginning with the departure of baby boomers,[6] church attendance and affiliation has declined considerably in white congregations. White Protestants were a slight majority segment in American culture as late as the 1970's. However, their numbers have steadily declined to the point that in 2014 the percentage dropped to 32%.[7] Curiously, ethnic Protestants, namely

---

[4] Bibby, *Resilient Gods*, 12. He's referencing old Gallup polls.
[5] PRRI, American Values Atlas, 2016. Accessed January 12 2018.
    http://ava.prri.org/#religious/2016/States/religion
[6] Bibby, *Resilient Gods*, 32.
[7] General Social Survey, 1974-2012; PRRI, American Values Atlas, 2013-2014
    Accessed January 18, 2018. http://ava.prri.org/

black and Hispanics, have not experienced the same losses (Hispanics in fact gaining during recent years).[8] This means the disintegration of Christendom is largely a result of the white Protestant
church losing its own members and failing to replace them. The
shifting source of power may not seem obvious, given the ongoing
influence of the white Protestant church, particularly conservative
branches closely tied to political parties, but that's because power
structures take time to change. We know, however, demographics
have already changed, and with it the overall influence of a church
that has lost its position at the center of society.

Although only the powerful can lose their power, all of Christianity has lost prominence, regardless of tradition, and therefore
everyone can discover a renewed sense of mission and adventure
in their unique context. Everyone needs to figure out ways to move
forward because even while church culture has lost adherents,
broader culture continues to trek forward. This is important because it changes what the average person thinks and believes. For
one, they no longer connect with the assumptions the church has
grown used to. It's these people we need to learn more about: those
who left the church decades ago, and those who were never there
to begin with.

The Nones

In North America, the largest growing religious segment is in fact
no religion at all. Sociologists refer to this segment—those who
claim no religious affiliation—as the religious "nones." Household
census data in Canada from 2011 reports this number at nearly a

---

[8] Ibid.

quarter (23.9%) of the population.[9] Pick any poll or sociology paper and the percentage is creeping up to 1/3 of total population. It's worth noting these are numbers describing religious affiliation. It doesn't mean everyone not a "none" goes to a church service. Actual weekly attendance is around 20%. The number of religious nones in America today hovers around a quarter of the population as well.[10] This number grows by about one percentage point a year. To extrapolate this trend plainly, half of Americans will claim no religious affiliation by 2040. This shift will happen in one generation.

Who are the Nones?

Hanging on my dining room wall is a cross a little larger than my hand. Reflecting Coptic designs, the St. George's cross is a unique piece made out of silver I purchased in Ethiopia. One day I had guests over and the conversation turned to the cross where I shared the story about its acquisition. My friend casually responded, "A cross? I thought it was a key."

I had the same remark when I prepping communion. After laying out the bread and wine, I added some ornaments including a vial of olive oil and a cross on the table. Because our church includes many unbelievers, the communion table is foreign to some. A friend approached as I was setting up, set his eyes on the display, and remarked, "Where did you get that key!?" pointing to the cross.

Then there's the young woman who was having trouble mak-

---

[9] Statistics Canada, National Household Survey, 2011.

[10] "Nones' on the Rise," *Religion & Public Life*, *Pew Research Center, October 9, 2012*, *http://www.pewforum.org/2012/10/09/nones-on-the-rise/*; Daniel Cox and Robert P. Jones, "America's Changing Religious Identity." PRRI. Accessed March 10th, 2018. https://www.prri.org/research/american-religious-landscape-christian-religiously-unaffiliated/

ing sense of a word. She poked her hand up to alert the professor. "What do you mean by the word 'sin?'" She needed some context. This wasn't an elementary Sunday school class, rather a university course on the history of the Reformation. Sin. A word ubiquitously known within the walls of Christendom for centuries is now obscure to an emerging generation. The nones have little to no religious memory because they didn't grow up with a church informing their lives. Chances are, their parents never went to a church either. They have grown up secular, and although most have visited a church building for a wedding or two, any meaningful connection with religion should no longer be assumed. Their world has little connection with religious stories, symbols, or even language. Because religion has no assumed place in their lives, the nones don't think to search for answers to life's questions at a church. To use a Biblical analogy, the nones are the children of the prodigal son if he never returned home.[11]

The Dones

If the nones describe a segment that has no religious connection, the dones describe people who grew up connected to a religious culture and have now chosen to abandon that religious influence in their daily lives. The dones used to go to church and therefore have some nascent understanding of the culture, language, symbols, and stories from Christendom. This is why one of the reasons well resourced churches focus heavily on young family programming: the potential of re-attracting the dones back into the fold. It's a viable way to pad the stats, but it's still not addressing the underlying issue: the church is becoming incompetent at communicating our dream

---

[11] Shout out to Connie Jakab, who got this idea as a "download" from God.

for better—the gospel—in a way the growing minority can even understand.

Spiritual But Not Religious

Here's what the nones and dones aren't by default—they aren't against religion. Which means they're certainly not against Jesus. Nones shouldn't be conflated with atheism, although atheists would certainly be categorized as nones. They are merely unaffiliated with religion. Many are neutral with religion (although most all of them have a problem with the conservative Christianity seen in mainstream media).[12] Most are what sociologists label "SBNR"—spiritual but not religious. This means despite declining church affiliation, it's not accurate to claim society is less spiritual. The dones and nones are open to spirituality. We all share an innate human quality regardless of religious affiliation. All bear the image of God and have root longings regardless of how we try to fill them. What we now see, however, is that traditional Christianity is no longer the first choice to meet the spiritual needs. In a "spiritual but not religious" worldview, the Christian faith (from message, to living) does have its attractive points.[13] But for the most part the world has shifted to new messaging on how to live life: online personalities, daytime talk shows, and TED talks. During this time, the institutional church has struggled to make incremental changes in the wake of massive cultural shifts. The result? The church is losing. It's fumbling with change because it doesn't know how to operate without the power and prestige of Christendom. In the meantime, the world carries on. As Bob Dylan lamented, the times are a-changing.

---

[12] Again, Bibby's latest book has a section that describes the perceptions of various faith traditions amongst a wide array of groups. Conservative evangelicals scored the lowest, just below Islam.

[13] Moreau, *Contextualization in World Missions*, 36.

Chapter 4

Our Mess &
How We Got Here

"*We are prophets of a future not our own.*"
- Bishop Untener on the Romero prayer.

*W*hen combined, the dones and nones are the largest religious segment in North America. They are unaffiliated, many possess some kind of prior connection to religion, and most are interested in spiritual things. If you can't hear it yet, let me be clear: this is a profound *opportunity* for the church. What's stopping us from embracing change tomorrow and throwing all we have into connecting with these new cultural segments? It has something to do with Darrel Guder's comments on the North American church. "Churches in America have become so accommodating to the American way of life that they are now domesticated, and it is no longer obvious what justifies their existence in particular communities."[14]

Before substantive changes can happen, an immobilizing force needs to be overcome—the illusion that existing church culture is working and worth keeping. It is, after all, easier to stay safe and

---

[14] Guder, *"Missional Church"*, 78.

ignore change, which is why most ideas die before seeing the light
of day. Ideas fall short because the problem is too big, the tension
too high, and the journey too risky. We think we're better off making the short-term and safe choice of preserving "the way it's always
been." But that's not the way it should be.

The State of Decline

The late Michael Spencer garnered significant attention in 2009
after writing a series on the decline in evangelicalism. He was exposing what many were too afraid to acknowledge at the time: the

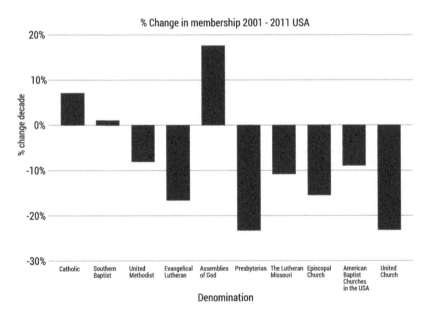

Figure 1. % Change in membership 2001-2011 in the USA. Data derived from eleven years
of number sets (2001-2012) published in, Yearbook of American & Canadian Churches, ed
Eileen W. Lindner (Nashville, Abingdom Press).

imminent collapse of evangelicalism in America.[15] This was of particular interest because white evangelicals represented the largest and most powerful religious segment in America. Spencer predicted that within a decade evangelicalism would collapse. His blog post turned into a Newsweek article that catalyzed feverish dialogue. "It can't be true," leaders declared after reading the dire warning. At the time of this book's publishing, Spencer's decade is almost up, and although evangelicalism is still around, the decline continues. We haven't experienced a cataclysmic end, but we have experienced a consistent slowing of church growth over the last sixty years. For example, Figure 1 depicts the top 10 denominations in America by membership (self-reported numbers). All but three declined in the period between 2001-2011. Which three? Catholics, Assembly of God, and the Southern Baptist Convention.

In that same period, all but one experienced multiple years of membership declines.[16] The data does not include independent denominations and mega churches. Nonetheless, decreases in church memberships are happening. The most recent data from most all statistics polls confirms Christian affiliation is declining, albeit slowly, as total population increases.[17] Lifeway Research is one of the few firms that would argue against abject decline, instead reporting increases in membership for some evangelical churches,

---

[15] Michael Spencer, "My Prediction: The Coming Evangelical Collapse (1)," *Internet Monk* January 27 2009, http://www.internetmonk.com/archive/my-prediction-the-coming-evangelical-collapse-1

[16] That one denomination was the Assemblies of God. They have boasted continued year-over-year growth over the past 25 years according to their own statistics (from 2016). You can find their data on their website: https://ag.org/About/Statistics

[17] Primary statistics agencies including PRRI, Pew Research, and Gallup. For example, this recent Gallup update on 2017 religious trends in America: Frank Newport, "America's Changing Religious Identity." Gallup, March 10th, 2018, https://www.prri.org/research/american-religious-landscape-christian-religiously-unaffiliated/.

particularly ones that have robust church planting strategies. It's their research that's determined statements like, "we close more churches than we plant," are false. However, they have not been able to demonstrate whether or not new churches are able to make up the difference for lost Christian affiliates, or if they primary rely on attracting lapsed or existing Christians to fill the pews. I assert that few, including evangelicals and their church planting efforts, are successfully connecting and finding new converts in a post-Christian world.

Take a look at your own denominational numbers over the past few years. (If you report an increase, I will challenge this assertion later.) What about your own church? The evidence, coupled with your own reality, reveals a church with dwindling membership, few newcomers, and unable to connect with people who don't look like them. This is the current state.

Staying Put

Churches respond to cultural shifts in a variety of ways, but often it's in opposition to change. Here are some common postures:

1. ignore and avoid culture shifts and become obsolete (splintered denominations);
2. try to convince the changing world to conform to them (defensive conservatives);
3. imitate culture by creative exclusive sub-culture (contemporary churches);
4. change on whim to accommodate every new culture (some mainline and liberal);
5. innovate to co-lead in post-Christendom.

I often hear about new church strategies that seek to build "resilience." But resilience only means weathering the storm. I'm more interested in churches, ideas, and the people who want to breathe fresh life into dry bones and thrive in a new culture. To get there, more churches need to embody the fifth posture—leading in post-Christendom. Sadly, I can't think of many churches today that fall into the category of innovating and leading in their neighborhood and city. If we're honest, most of us are stuck somewhere between one and four. That's not to suggest churches should not exist in these categories. Orthodox traditions have little interest in reaching beyond their ethnic boundaries. Other faith traditions are committed to retaining their "way of life" at all costs. But my concern is when the majority of churches operate in a posture of either creating sub-cultures for Christians to hide in, or substitute culture that look no different from mainstream. We need ideas that reach beyond our borders. But resistance to new ideas keeps holding us back from making the switch. During this time, the critical problem remains: Christianity in the West is disintegrating and signs point to continuous decline. That's probably not shocking news to you, but what shocks me is how casual our response has been. For many, it's still not a big enough problem to forgo existing comfort in favor of profound shifts. We've been pre-occupied with maintaining our "normal," at the cost of potentially losing it all. For others, they know something needs to be done, but so far the attempts have fallen flat (if we make any at all). Those that try also know there's so much resistance when even a glimmer of an idea confronts the comfortable ordinary. Despite how grand ideas may seem, we need significant and compelling reasons to justify sacrificing our safety to live them out. We need to know that the risk to stay outweighs the cost to leave.

Not Marginalized

Churches and denominations working to reclaim their power over culture by relying on legislation to protect ideologies and beliefs are also those who claim their version of Christianity is being threatened by the growth of secularism and pluralism. But the data doesn't support the argument. Christianity is not under "threat" from other religions, despite the prejudice against other world religions like Islam. World Christian Encyclopedia estimates that by 2025 non-Christian religions will account for a minuscule 7% of total population in the United States.[18] The decline of Christianity will square off against non-religious affiliation, not other faith traditions. Secularism, or the rise of the nones and dones, is different, with the majority of culture swaying towards no religious affiliation. But as I noted earlier, no religious affiliation doesn't mean anti-religion. Atheist affiliation itself is a small percentage of the population.[19] So why is it some Christians fear they're being marginalized? It seems how they deal with the loss of inherited privilege is the real issue at hand.

The loss of Christendom pushes the church to the cultural margins, but that shouldn't be confused with marginalization. Those who fail to innovate see cultural shifts as a major threat to existence because it is. It's true, privilege is eroding, yet marginalization can't be claimed by the one losing privilege. It's merely losing privilege. How you survive and thrive within a different culture is the question we are asking, not how we can reclaim an old position at the top.

---

[18] Barrett, *World Christian Encyclopedia*, 772.

[19] Numbers will vary based on region. Generally self-identified "atheists" come in under 10%, and likely closer to 5%. Consult Bibby for Canadian numbers and Pew Research for American.

The Abbey

The first time I visited Europe I spent time in the heart of Paris, London, Brussels, and Edinburgh. Each city offers a vast array of cultural experiences offering visceral connections to the voices of those who've gone before. There's no shortage of history, particularly church history.

One form of "liturgy" I tried in every city was to visit as many churches as possible. The anti-cathedral designs of my native evangelical culture produced plain warehouse boxes in far away suburbs. Old cathedrals, on the other hand, were immersive spiritual experiences. I marvelled at every monument and stained glass scene I could soak in. But not everyone felt the same way. Regardless of which city I was in there were commonalities. European churches, outside of service times, sat empty inside. Ironically, during the day, they acted as informal meeting spaces on the outside. Young people gathered together on the outside steps to hangout. I thought to myself, so close yet so far. One of the most heartbreaking, but ironically pleasant, things I noticed about the popular churches: Notre Dame, St Paul's, or Westminster Abby all had massive tourist line-ups to visit the interior. Two hour waits and a surcharge to enter. Not a fan of long waits, I discovered a couple of ways to beat the crowd. Clergy can usually enter at a discount and at a separate entrance. But once inside you still have to herd your way through. The second revelation, and a testament to the state of Christianity in Europe as a whole, are times you can visit for free when it's relatively empty, and you can spend hours soaking in your encounter. All you have to do is go during a worship service. No line, no cover charge, and it comes complete with a free organ performance. To me, participating in the rhythmic Anglican liturgy was a cathartic worship moment that made me forget the regular parishioners were over the age of 70 and were outnumbered by visiting tourists 7 to 1. One summer day as I sat in Westminster Abbey, droplets of rain cascaded down the Gothic buttresses, whilte the deep bellows of the church organ filled the sanctuary and the senses. The choir sang Psalm 88,

> *"O Lord God of my salvation, I have cried day and night before thee: O let my prayer enter into thy presence, incline thine ear unto my calling."*

My brief time visiting European churches was a looking glass into the future of the North American church: empty, save for the few aging faithful. How will we respond? Do our dreams connect into the epic tale that beckons the entirety of creation into reconciliation? We need to know we can't force outside culture to change for the church. We can only change ourselves. That means it's our responsibility to translate our faith for those who will listen, hear, and see it in action. Implicitly or explicitly, churches have expected outsiders to come to us. It's not working. We cannot expect the problem to meet us in our own world, in our own language, looking for our pre-packaged solutions. Our cities no longer seek the church for answers to important questions like: What's my calling in life? Or why love? In Christendom, most people had connection to Christianity and the stories. All the church had to do was remind them of their lapse. Today we're in trouble because we are running out of people to remind. If that doesn't seem like a significant problem then there's one more step to dismantle: the vanity of certaintyand security attached to the contemporary church.

Chapter 5

Goldilocks Church

"We used to look up at the sky and wonder at our place in the stars,
now we just look down and worry about our place in the dirt."
- Cooper, from the film "Interstellar"

*I*t took some convincing before Bilbo reluctantly agreed to join the adventure posed by Gandalf. Initially, he didn't want to leave the routine and comfort of the Shire. Luke Sykwalker wasn't sure he was ready to accept Obi-Wan's suggestion to begin his training at the academy. Prospective heroes start off stubborn and lazy. That's why they reject their initial call. After all, life is easier in the familiar world. The inertia built by a culture of individualism is a powerful force that keeps many planted in a safe routine. Human nature desires the path of least resistance because we're hardwired for preservation. That's why we need profound reasons to overcome resistance to settle. For this to happen, we need proof the adventure is going to be worth the cost, and the problem we face is big enough to warrant the risk.

It's normal to ask these questions too. You *should* wrestle with, "Why would I risk a successful ministry, job security, or my career in the church?" Before committing in full to a new idea, especially ones that challenge the status quo, we need to be shaken to the core. Your church is not immune to decline, nor are the churches who claim to be growing. Although you may boast ministries, discipleship, small groups, outreach, missions, etc., that work on the surface, deep down there may be an issue.

The Ruse

By popular measurements it's a success. Your church boasts steady attendance, the odd newcomer, and a solid volunteer base supporting ministries. But that's the inside. How are you connecting with people who don't fit your *gold leaf standard*? The ones who don't look like you and don't fit your culture? There's nothing wrong with providing strong programs to existing Christians. Our problem with the decline has to do with a church that devotes the bulk of resources to the delivery of Christian programs (the Sunday service).

Pastor Jon, from our average church in Chapter 2, wasn't thinking, "My church is dying." He's a reflection of contemporary church leaders, largely focused internally—at the expense of foresight—on how the loss of Christendom affects the local church body. His church was good at maintaining the world they were comfortable with. As a result it was rare to see non-Christians in the community. Would you call his church a success?

The Current State

I want to make some broad observations here. I can't capture everyone, but I'll capture most. Your church is part of the downward trend of decline and likely falls into one of these categories.

1. A church or denomination where you have no choice. You've waited too long to face decline that's been happening for decades. At this point you'll try anything because you're literally facing the brink. Within a generation, apart from the benefit of significant

endowments, mainline churches won't be able to keep the doors open. The mainline churches are selling church buildings because there's no revenue for upkeep because of the loss, sometimes up to 90%, of adherents.[20] Some are trying to reinvent the wheel within their realm of traditionalism but are quickly realizing it's too little too late.

2. An average size congregation of around 100, that could balance this status quo for the foreseeable future. Some are aware of outside culture shifts and are asking tough questions about the future of the congregation. Others are content to protect their corner of a shrinking sandbox. These churches rarely add to their congregations through conversion.

3. An ethnic congregation where everyone literally looks the same, and there's little interest to change or try new things beyond ethnic boundaries. You may be able to maintain your numbers by relying on new immigrants. The second or third generations are starting to feel the disconnect and are leaving.

4. Lastly, we have a large church that appears resilient or even growing. They are bucking the trend of decline. Something appears to be working, at least on the surface. Let's dig deeper to find out.

Ministry Pornography

One of the reasons churches have failed to notice the magnitude of their lost connection with the outside world is called *church exceptionalism*. One day I was having lunch with a leader working in the national office for an organization doing traditional mission but in a local context. We discussed how smaller churches try to emulate wildly successful models from bigger churches. He took

---

[20] For example, the United Church of Canada.

the analogy one step further, calling church exceptionalism *ministry pornography*.[21] Leaders look upon the best and brightest stars (other pastors) of the biggest or fastest growing churches, and figure out what strategies and tactics they can copy. However, there's a danger when smaller churches look to their larger counterparts for inspiration. To use business terminology, the small mom-and-pop outfit can't emulate the national corporation. They can't replicate the same strategies and efforts, and if they try, they won't capture the same results.

Large churches ask different questions than small ones, such as: strategies needed to scale, organizational efficiency, governance, staff management, individual experience, budgets, vision, and strategic implementation. Conversely, smaller churches will ask questions on how to respond faster to local needs, will value moving slow, and will take time to incarnate in the neighborhood, decentralize leadership, increase participation in mission, and hopefully spend more time in depth of relationship. All this says how you lead and live out your dream is entirely dependent on your context. The appeal to find quick answers is attractive. Yet in our desperation to find a solution, a level of cognitive dissonance emerges where leaders fail to ask one simple question: do those exceptional churches actually grow? The short answer is, not really.

Goldilocks

It is true that exceptional evangelical churches do boast resilient congregations, albeit only in comparison to other traditions. In their book, A *Culture of Faith*, Sam Reimer and Michael Wilkinson

---

[21] Likely an idea inspired by Eugene Peterson, *Under the Unpredictable Plant. An Exploration in Vocational Holiness* (Grand RapidsL Willian B. Eerdmans, 1992), 22-25.

suggest this reason: the maintenance of strong subcultures balanced to be different enough from the "world," but not too different from broad cultural norms.[22] For example, evangelicals hold particular views regarding marriage, biblical authority, and sexuality, yet adopt technology in services, and condone the privatization that appeals to the quintessential consumer Christian. The result is a cycle where leaders cater to consumer Christianity by offering the "Goldilocks" experience. Think of it as the "lukewarm" Church of Laodicea.[23] They were severely admonished for their culture. This church was so lost they even locked Jesus out of their church gatherings! Like the Laodiceans, Goldilocks churches create an internal culture that's not too hot and not too cold. If they challenge parishioners too much over discipleship or nationalism or women and ministry, parishioners may leave for the church down the road. Don't challenge enough and people may leave for deeper "biblical preaching." Rather than upset the balance, the sub-culture of the Goldilocks Church maintains environments that are "just right" for the primary demographic.

Not-So-Exceptional

As a whole, resilient or growing churches are not growing by evangelism. I don't want to diminish "growing" churches, but the claim is worth examining in detail. A closer look reveals exceptional churches aren't all they claim to be. This is an important observation to make. To find success in post-Christendom, we need to confront other ideas that precent necessary change from happening.

When we dig into data, churches from the past 20 years that

---

[22] Reimer and Wilkinson, *A Culture of Faith*, Chapter 2.
[23] Revelation 3:14-22.

added members did so through three primary and nearly exclusive ways.[24]

1. Christians switching from other churches.
2. Births in the existing congregation.
3. Christian immigrants.

Churches that claim growth do so by adding existing Christians. These three primary growth sources reveal why well resourced churches are "growing."

1. They can afford robust programming for new immigrants, or they have developed expertise in launching ethnic congregations targeted to new immigrants and underserved ethnic populations.
2. They are the largest and by default have the most births.
3. They provide excellence in music, preaching, and young family programming.

Not to dissuade existing church planting or innovative church expressions, but there are strategic ways to grow a new church without the need for many new converts. The Assemblies of God, the single denomination that's experienced consistent growth year-over-year for the past 25 years certainly see many new converts (perhaps among the highest number of any major denomination), but also rely on their expertise building ethnic congregations to appeal to underserved demographics. Catholic membership increases depends on new immigrants of existing Catholics. SBC has a robust

[24] Reimer & Wilkinson, *A Culture of Faith.*

church planting network but relies heavily on Christian transfers to get moving. There is expertise within each, however, they are not primarily geared towards a post-Christian context.

The three primary growth mechanisms also make it hard for smaller churches to grow, especially if they try to replicate exceptional churches. Small can't match the programming resources and therefore lose members to the very model they're trying to emulate. It results in frustrating stagnation, slow losses that deflate momentum, and the continued monotony of managing an unmovable flock.

Did you notice what's missing from the list of three? Reimer and Wilkinson asked congregants in evangelical churches what they thought the highest priorities in their churches were.[25] Evangelism was one of the lowest ranked. Targeted family programming for members was the highest. Despite the hype to grow by evangelism, few churches do. The intentions are there, but the results are not. Exceptional churches, the ones others look to for answers because they appear to grow, *don't grow by evangelism.* The current trajectory is still decline or at best maintaining the already churched. So what's the answer? To address the decline we need new followers. How this can be done is the next question. The solutions we seek for robust discipleship or evangelism don't seem to exist in the exceptional churches. To find some answers we have to explore *why* we're in trouble: the church is disintegrating because we've forgotten our mission. I believe we need a re-orientation in thinking and in practice surrounding our whole approach to mission and the church. Fix the function of mission, then watch the church grow.

Kodak Moment

---

[25] Reimer and Wilkinson, *A Culture of Faith*, 101.

Kodak was the industry juggernaut for all things film, but in 2012, they declared bankruptcy. The story of Kodak is one of catastrophic failure because they did not recognize the magnitude of a technology they invented 30 years prior. Kodak owned the early digital camera but refused to acknowledge it as a threat to business because they were comfortable and content with their monopoly on film. The old saying, "where you settle, there you die," rang true for a company that chose to ignore change they saw coming because it was too disruptive to the familiar ordinary. They disregarded the threat and missed an opportunity. Their choice wound up driving the company out of business.

The church is currently in a Kodak moment. We may choose to ignore the warning signs of culture change but at what future cost? Are we content to do nothing more than protect what's left? Would we have greater urgency if we knew the slow decline is leading to catastrophic failure? These are questions we must consider as we struggle with the tension of normal human desires to self-preserve and stay safe. Turning ideas real is risky. But there's also an equally compelling force within our being: an urge to pioneer something new and turn ideas real. Deep down we know staying put prevents the change required for future survival.

Enough with the bad news. What can we do to fix the problem?

Part II.

Returning to the Source

"Where we re-build the
necessary foundation."

Chapter 6

Purpose of Call

"In the same way, let your light shine before others, that they
may see your good deeds and glorify your Father in heaven."
- Matthew 5:16 (NIV).

Remember the answer to build a church that thrives in a new post-Christian culture? It relies on building, or releasing, the gifts of the church. The potential of the people needs to be unlocked. That's where this section comes in. It aims to add shape, definition, and re-orientation to the key factors of identity and mission that builds a church capable of co-creating alongside culture. This chapter is divided into three parts. First, understanding the breadth of God's mission and how it acts as the source and purpose for all things. Second, discovering the base of our individual callings and identity. Third, connecting this identity to the callings given to the body and how these necessary structures support turning our dreams real.

First: The Missio Dei

It starts with the Triune God hovering over the waters of creation, a primal activity that reveals the heart of God's character. God dwelled in the Garden, chased after the banished, made a promise to Abraham, encountered Moses in the desert, sent priests, prophets, and kings, ultimately sent his Son, then the Spirit, and now the church. This is only a snapshot of the entire narrative, but in this glimpse we capture a theme of sending activity. Missiologists use the theological term *missio Dei* (Latin for "mission of God"), as a reference to this activity in the grand story that starts in the Garden and ends with the New Garden in the New City (Revelation 22). This story at its heart reveals what the *missio Dei* in past, present, and future is about: God is a sending God seeking to rescue and redeem all of creation.

The *missio Dei* doesn't belong to the church nor is it your own. It is decidedly God's and we are invited to participate in the unfolding plan. God does not merely own mission, rather it is a fundamental *attribute* of God.[26] The distinction is important. Mission as *missio Dei* seeks to shift what was once a component of missiology, soteriology, or ecclesiology, into the heart of Trinitarian theology and the very nature of God. Today, however, the mission has been diminished.

When you hear the word "mission" what is the first thing that crosses your mind? (It might be useful to consider what the average person in your community thinks as well.) Mission is often treated as an offshoot ministry of the church. It represents separate work we do in a special "missions week," support through parachurch organizations, or short-term trips. Many assume doing mission work requires specialized expertise and is characterized in two different extremes: evangelistic efforts done by missionaries in a foreign land, or work done for social improvement. But neither represents the breadth and magnitude of God's mission. Rather, we need to approach mission—the *missio Dei*—as a lens through which

---

[26] Bosch, *Transforming Mission*, 400.

we view our faith and function.

From the catalytic work of missiologist Lesslie Newbigin; The Gospel and our Culture Network; and Darryl Guder's seminal compilation, *Missional Church*, emerged a movement that seeks to re-new mission activity. "Missional church" aims to re-orient our understanding and function of mission in the Western church. From Christendom, the church assumed a static posture on mission: sending missionaries into the world. In post-Christendom, mission must recapture God's original intent by not merely sending a few, but building the entire body with the identity of being *sent ones*. The missional oriented church seeks to release every person to live out their dreams for better, connected into God's mission to rescue and redeem all of creation. How can we work towards building a community of sent ones?

Second: Calling and Identity

A cataclysmic bang—or perhaps it was just a whisper—set the cosmos in motion, and innumerable stars and planets filled a vast nothing. Out of the ordered chaos a tiny blue planet emerged. First, it rested formless and void of any living thing, but then its purpose slowly took shape. New pieces were added age by age from the sky, the waters, the plants, the animals, and built towards the pinnacle moment—the creation of humanity.

One day out of the ground man emerges. Eerily from his rib woman is formed. The vast created order was overshadowed by these two significant characters, declared "very good" compared to all of the rest. Their uniqueness was defined in their identity: *image bearers made in the likeness of the Creator.*

The opening scene ends with a celebrated time of hallowed rest. Although it was fleeting, the significance of this fragment in time means everything. In this moment we glimpse God's ultimate hope for creation—the time when all things are right. Shalom. The day of rest glimpses our hope of creation in harmony with its Creator. In this book I use *God's dream* and the *kingdom of God* interchangeably to refer to this final hope. The *missio Dei* is the road to experience the fullness of this dream today, and glimpses the hope coming to completion tomorrow.

Building an identity as sent ones begins when we establish our human identity as image bearers. It's a revelation that not only have we been created in the image of God, but that God would care to know your name and call you son or daughter. From here we can add pieces that capture the heart of God's mission in our own lives. How? If we want to know more about the character of God, we look at Jesus. Jesus revealed the epitome of God's mission in incarnation. Incarnation is the awesome reality that God contextualized himself to touch, feel, smell, and sympathize with your weaknesses. God incarnated to be present, and is still present with us. That presence lives in us now and calls us to some specific characteristics. Namely, living out the fullness of our humanity as image bearers of the Creator. As Ross Hastings says, "the telos of the Christian mission is thus human beings becoming fully human."[27]

Commission and Commandments

Jesus provides foundations for his followers in the gospels. He defines our mission by naming the source of his in the commission found in John's Gospel: "As the Father sent me, I am sending you."[28] Sent to do what? *Join the missio Dei bearing witness to the hope here*

---

[27] Ross Hastings, "Missional God, Missional Church. Hope for Re-Evangelizing the West." Downers Grove: InterVarsity Press, 2012.14.

and now of final restoration yet to come. At the end of Matthew's Gospel the Great Commission is delivered to the disciples: go into all of the nations to baptize and teach. Although intentional witness and evangelism are components of this commission, God's mission goes deeper than evangelism. These commissions are woven under the wider commission found in Genesis 1-2 describing our role as sub-creators on earth. We discover the fullness of our humanity when we adopt the commission to live out to the world the redemptive activity first seen in God through Christ. What that practically looks like is built into the Greatest Command.

Only one commandment is called great. Christians are fundamentally defined by embodiment of the Great Commandment to simply and profoundly *love*. The commandment to love comes in four parts.

1. Love the Lord your God with all of your heart, life, and mind (Matthew 22:37);
2. Bear witness through your love for one another (John 15:12-15);
3. Love your neighbor (Matthew 22:39);
4. Love yourselves (Matthew 22:39).

The love that we share as Christians is our crucial witness to God's hope. It's a kind of love that knows no bounds, goes all the way to the very end where no one else will go, and then goes one step more. If we don't get the foundation of love right, everything built on top will emerge off of shaky ground. That doesn't mean we don't continuously struggle to love, but it should remain *the* central

---

[28] John 20:21 (NIV).

identifying factor in and about our churches. How we love means looking and acting like Jesus in all that we do and believe. He is the pinnacle of God's mission to rescue and restore all of creation. He is the Messiah who inaugurates this kingdom on Earth. It is through his actions, by death and resurrection, that God delivers the answer to the original hope glimpsed in the Garden and promised to Abraham.[29]

But we're caught in the in-between too. We have the fullness of God's hope inaugurated in Christ, but that hope still hasn't fully been realized. Bad things still happen in our world. Evil still exists. We're caught in a "now but not yet" of the kingdom, and this is where the next component exists. The church becomes the primary body to act as witnesses to the hope that has come and will come again.[30] Let's unpack this calling to the church.

Third: The Church in Ephesus

We start again with Jesus, who is the head of the church body (Colossians 1:15-20), and shapes overall church function by demonstrating the practical ways we should live (the love commandment). Tasked to bear witness to Christ's character, the church is also given this clear calling in Ephesians 4:

> *"You must live up to the calling you received. Bear with one another in love; be humble, meek, and patient in every way with one another. Make every effort to guard the unity that the spirit gives, with your life bound together in peace"*

---

[29] This is a truncated explanation of Christ's faithfulness to God's purpose for Israel. I recommend reading NT Wright's, The Day the Revolution Began, for a near complete insight.

[30] Acts 1:6-8

- Ephesians 4:2-3, Kingdom New Testament.

Let's begin in verse two: *"bear with one another in love; be humble, meek, and patient in everyday with one another. Make every effort to guard the unity that the spirit gives...."* This is what we should look like. As we set out to live out our dreams for better, the first step is living out the love for one another with a character of humbleness, meekness, and patience.

Why should we live out this character? Because of the identity we derive from God. The ensuing verses four to six articulate the source in the form of one of the earliest church creeds: *"...one body, spirit, baptism, God and father of all, who is over all, through all, and in all."*

Now to application and how the church can actively live out its identity. The people are given gifts to fulfil this task. Some are called to be *apostles,* others *prophets, evangelists, pastors* (shepherds), and *teachers.*[31] Some suggest every person has all the pieces, some suggest only one or two. Some suggest only four gifts exist, others five.[32] Verse seven is worth emphasizing too: *"...grace was given to each one of us."* The gifts given to the church (the people) include everyone. No parameters exist in this chapter that qualify gifts based on gender.

Stop for a moment and reflect on your local church. Can you clearly identify people in your congregation based on these gifts? You might be able to pick out the popular gifts like pastor or teacher, but apostles and prophets are harder. We also tend to label leaders with these gifts, rather than building the body to discover their own. A church that leaves the bulk of responsibility and activity

---

[31] There are additional gifts described in Romans 12 and 1 Corinthians 12.

[32] The APEST model from Ephesians 4 has been developed extensively in the missional church conversation. For example, consult the work of Alan Hirsch and Mike Frost. Hirsch has written extensively on scripture, theology, and practical training for this model.

in the hands of the qualified few reduces its strength. It becomes ineffective at engaging the fullness of mission because the gifts of the body are dormant in the pews. Christians should actively cultivate their gifts, and pursue the calling they've received. All five gifts build the body, yet more often than not, in practice giftings like evangelist are sent "to the field"; apostles are the entrepreneurs who don't fit; and the prophets are hard to welcome because they constantly disturb the status quo. Yet we need all gifts if the church is to embody the fullness of its call. Your dream won't have success without the combination of these gifts in action.

However you approach the gifts in Ephesians 4, analyze whether the function of your church develops the body, or merely works to retain power for those already in charge (maintenance of the institution). Ultimately, the church should produce the result found in verse 13—the *building* of the body. Does your church invite and disciple people and their gifts? And is the result the building of the body? When we disciple people well, the community reflects newness of resurrected life. From there the fruit of our ministry—the building of the body—is our work away from the decay in our world and into the fullness of new life found in Jesus. The church gathers to live out this new humanity that pursues justice, love, and genuine holiness. Is this happening in your community?

Re-Imagining Local Mission

The building of the body isn't a push to build a particular brand or denomination. God's kingdom knows no bounds. In post-Christendom we need to find allies in the kingdom, and not just those who wear the denominational logo. The church as a whole is invited to be a major participant in God's hope for the world, yet our footprint is decreasing because the way we tell the story is lost in translation to a non-church culture. This despite non-churchgoers longing for the same kind of restoration offered through the Gospel. The question is, do current institutional structures accommodate the necessary shifts?

Despite the function in Ephesians 4, in practice, the bulk of most church activity and messaging is reliant on a Sunday service that no longer appeals to outsiders. Most of our gatherings look like this: five songs, announcements, 30-45 minute sermon, song. Week in and week out. What we value is shown in our posture, where we spend time and money, activities that define what our communities are about. In a declining environment, it seems we pour energy into delivering services, and build an identity of congregations that plateau at volunteering. Does this sound like a church participating in the wholeness of God's hope of restoration? A church designed to release people with their gifts to join God's mission? A people living out the character of Jesus in their neighborhoods and beyond?

What happens if we return to our purpose as church and as individuals? What happens if we return to the founding platform of mission? This church looks different as it shifts its design and activities to embrace and build the gifts of *all*. It is a church that joins an already unfolding mission that may not describe everything it does (we still worship with one another), but it does describe everything the church is sent to do in the world.[33] Sent ones embodying love for God, one another, and the other. Sent ones that glimpse a preview of heaven now—a hope that all brokenness in our midst will one day be restored.

---

[33] Stott, *Christian Mission in the Modern World*, 23.

Chapter 7

The Crossroads

---

*"Go therefore and make disciples of all the nations, baptizing them
in the name of the Father and of the Son and of the Holy Spirit,
teaching them to observe all things that I have commanded you;
and lo, I am with you always, even to the end of the age.' Amen"*
- Matthew 28:19-20 (NKJV)

*H*e's standing at a vast empty crossroads deciding what road he'll
choose next. Dust billows in the air as the options swirl in his
mind. Options. For the first time in what feels like a lifetime he
can choose his own fate. There was a time, five years ago, when his
life was typical. The safety of a solid job, big house, beautiful wife,
hardly a life anyone would call adventurous. Then it all came to a
crashing halt....

In the movie "Castaway," Chuck Nolan, played by Tom Hanks,
is stranded on a remote Pacific island following a tragic plane crash.
Chuck survives for years using meager tools while relying on the
inanimate volleyball he named "Wilson" for company. Sustaining
him through his arduous quest were two lingering goals: return to
the longing embrace of his wife, and deliver an unopened FedEx
package that washed ashore with him.

Fast forward to the end of the film: Chuck miraculously survives his ordeal and returns home, but discovers everything has changed in his absence. The hope that compelled him through his miraculous return was a heartbreaking illusion. His wife remarried. He no longer owned his house or his car. Although he and his wife share a tearful reunion, he moves from the loneliness of a deserted island to a new kind of loneliness in a new old world. Chuck is left without his fairy-tale ending.

The last scene shows Chuck driving down a rural country road to deliver that unopened package he brought on his long journey home. Once the delivery was done, and his two goals complete, a blank slate loomed in front of him. The final shot of the film shows Chuck standing alone, car idling, staring at four empty roadways, contemplating where to go next. The screen fades to black....

Although the movie ends before we can find out, one thing is certain, Chuck didn't stay at the crossroads forever. In fact, he had no choice. *There was no return.* His only option was to choose a path and go. Like Chuck, the Western church is staring at a looming crossroads that beckons us to make a pressing decision. *Something needs to change.* It's time for you to take your dreams and ideas for better and make the attempt to see it through. That dream can't re-capture or re-live the past—we can never go back. The world the church once knew and ruled is gone. The only choice is to live out a dream that propels us forward.

Sailing

Picture three kinds of boats on the open seas, each representing a form of the contemporary church. The first is a boat without a sail, oars, or a motor. It's floating at the mercy of the ocean currents and has no control over its direction—which means it can't avoid looming storms bent on capsizing them. The second is a cruise ship, full of temporary passengers looking for the comforts of the world within the novelty of the sea. Outfitted with massive motors, the cruise ship ignores prevailing ocean currents to arrive at the chosen destination. The third ship is a sailboat, using its sails to crisscross the given winds to cut a path towards the eventual destination. The first boat is going to sink. The second boat will exist so long as there's a demand and that's fine. The third sailboat is what we need more of: outfits capable of seizing the prevailing winds of the day, changing directions in a flash, and racing towards the final goal.

Is your church living out heaven now and previewing the kingdom on earth by living out the character of Jesus in the neighborhoods? Are you repairing what's broken, righting systemic injustices, caring for the other, and fighting growing poverty in your city? Or are you stuck trying to save a familiar yet declining world? Do your activities retain the comforts of Christian culture at the cost of crippling your capability to faithfully live out your calling as participants in the unfolding reign of God in your cities and beyond? Here's the truth behind all of these questions: wherever you are in the journey, God invites you to participate deeper in the unfolding dream for creation. That means your ideas, along with your church and community, play an exciting role in the here and now. It's time to set the sails beyond the known comforts. Will you begin your journey to live out the *one* act, the *one* moment, the *one* choice to chase out the fullness of God's calling and turn your dreams and ideas real?

Part III.

Action Architecture

"Where we learn new ways forward."

Chapter 8

Ideas are
Worth Nothing

"An idea's not really an idea until it is expressed – and expressed in the fullest, most powerful, and most compelling form you can create."
- John Butman

*H*ave you ever stumbled on a product or service and exclaimed, "that was MY idea!" We all have million-dollar ideas that someone else "stole." But have you ever tried to turn your million-dollar idea real?

The Attempts

An entrepreneur is not measured on monetary success (although that's usually the goal), but on their ability to take ideas and turn them real. I've been an entrepreneur for my entire adult career. In the span of nearly 20 years I've started a couple of churches and countless different businesses. Most of them have been small web-based outfits, but others have paid off, including web marketing consulting, general contracting, and book publishing. In my work I've accomplished three things. First, I've identified business op-portunities, developed them, and eventually turned a profit. Sec-

ond, and more importantly, I've taken ideas and made them real.
I've tried and tested concepts to learn what works and could work.
The third and critical accomplishment I've made is I've failed—*a
lot*. (I'll talk specifically about failure later.) Ideas that didn't get off
the ground, some that did but failed right away, some that took off
but eventually collapsed, some that are in the slow burn to turn a
profit (like my first publication, an adult coloring book, *Soul Coats:
Restoration*), or the mound of opportunities I never took. In the
midst of these three features I've learned that, regardless of success,
the attempt matters most. Without consistent work to try new ideas,
there is no production of newness, no mechanism to inform future
endeavours with valuable insight, and no means to success.

If you want a crash course on what it takes to turn ideas into
a successful business, watch a few episodes of Dragon's Den (or
Shark Tank in the U.S.). The show puts wealthy investors in front
of business pitches from entrepreneurs looking for cash flow and
expansion. In exchange, the entrepreneurs give up assets, usually
in the form of sizeable percentages in their business, which also
means future profits. The caveat is the massive potential to make
far more profit with the help of a Dragon than without. One thing
is consistent on the show. If a business pitch piques the interest of
the investors, they will ask for the current revenue and sales numbers. If the result is unimpressive the investors usually decline the
pitch. It's also exceedingly rare to find a business that merely offers
an *idea*. Investors want to know the entrepreneur didn't need the
safety of somebody else's money before making an attempt. They
want to see proof of concept usually delivered in real sales. They
want to see the idea in action because *ideas without action are worth
nothing*.

In 2002, as online resources and e-commerce platforms were

emerging, I owned an online consumer forum on cell phones. At the time, any search query pertaining to the big cell phone companies in Canada (and some in the U.S.), would deliver my website. Although it had growing exposure there were two problems: I had no passion for cell phones, and the website didn't have a lot of useful information. (This made it frustrating when I had a question about my own cell phone and kept getting my website as the only search result.) I sold the website to the highest bidder and walked away from the potential, which could have rivalled the biggest consumer related website for tech and gadgets if I had that interest. Key phrase: could have.

I had another idea in 2004. I created a website with the purpose of featuring videos from the barely-there video capabilities of cell phones. There was an obvious gap in technology between videos you shot on your candy bar Nokia, and featuring them on the world wide web. The problem was twofold. Videos needed to be uploaded manually using a cord to the computer, and then to the net, and I had no passion for cell phones. Today, outside of data restrictions, you can post video snippets wherever there's cell coverage. The emergence of Vine, Snapchat, Instagram Stories, Twitter (Periscope), and Facebook Live are revolutionizing the way we communicate. Was it possible that my idea could have rivalled these social media giants? Absolutely not. Even if I had created a functioning website, I needed to be first to market, hold enough development dollars to maintain a working version, and have the resources to market amid major players. Plus the name *PhVid* (pronounced "fid") was lame. Could have....

The Switch Flips

Right out of seminary I was trying to find a church where I could fit. I had the skills to work in the contemporary evangelical church, but the worship and community experience left me feeling like I was neglecting part of my identity. I also sensed I wasn't responding to the fullness of my own calling. It has since taken me a while to find confidence in my own voice and call, but at the time I was searching for a place where I could live out my dreams and ideas. During that time church planting became a viable possibility. It certainly fit my entrepreneurial skill set. Long story short, after going through the process, the opportunity to be a denominationally supported church planter dissipated. One colleague suggested the way forward with the denomination would be to put my head down, attend one of the churches regularly, and build some more relationships. Fair enough, I thought, but there was one problem. The ideas I had for church didn't look anything like the common evangelical experience. I knew there was more to the common worship experience that I found particularly deflating. Nonetheless I tried, but I didn't last long.

It was baptism and Easter Sunday service in the school gym. I should've been—I don't know—joyful? But I wasn't. It was in that moment I had an epiphany of sorts. Before me were two choices. I could try to stay and go through the motions. If I did I felt certain I would lose my faith. The alternative was to move forward and try out the ideas I had for the church and the city. To strike out on my own would be risky and ill-advised (which I'll talk about later). There was no going back and staying in the middle of evangelicalism that wasn't growing and suffered from the problem of sameness.

Every idea encounters a moment when the switch flips from whimsical daydream coupled with procrastination, to belief and action. I hope by now you've noticed the theme with ideas. It's one thing to see problems today and merely acknowledge the merits of potential solutions. It's quite another to do something about it. Think about your daydream for better. Daydreaming about your invisible lottery winnings was proof you already have half of what it takes to turn ideas real in God's unfolding narrative. The other half? Anybody can daydream, but turning dreams real is what we're after. Living out your idea, even in the smallest of ways, counts big. Let's figure out ways to make it happen.

Chapter 9

Yes!
Send Me

"Whom shall I send? And who will go for us?"
- Isaiah 6:8 (NIV)

*B*efore I found myself questioning my faith in a typical medium sized suburban evangelical church, I attended a typical small neighborhood evangelical church until high school. I still remember our heyday when the church hovered around 100+ for a season. But for the most part it was around 55-70 every week. Being small, it offered me a lot of opportunity to try different ministry roles ranging from leading worship to launching an evening service. It also left a specific evangelical imprint on my faith that I took with me to university.

Around this time I had a distinct sense God was leading me into ministry. In what capacity, I wasn't clear, but pastoral leadership was something I was drawn to. It was a fit particularly for my gift mix as a natural leader. After I completed my economics degree, the next phase sent me to seminary. There my comfortable evangelical ordinary world encountered new ideas. My paradigm shifted—or should I say dismantled—then thankfully rebuilt. Today, I regard my seminary experience as one of the critical formation moments in my faith. That might seem ironic given how far my ministry wound up from institutional paradigms. Nonetheless, it was instrumental in challenging existing theological paradigms, and developed my current passion for church and culture. I owe most of my direction and focus to the time and relationships developed during my three-year stay.

By the end of seminary I was looking for a job and had the skills to serve in the church well, including preaching, worship, and small group ministries. Although I was distinctly entrepreneurial in my career (I was, and still am, bi-vocational), I nonetheless sought a normal pastoral role. It was, after all, the safe plan. Despite my search the opportunities were slim. (Often new grads from Bible college or seminary will start low on the totem pole, usually in youth ministry, which is decidedly not a skill of mine.) One opportunity, however, did emerge: the possibility of becoming a church planter in the inner city. As an entrepreneur, and someone living in the urban center, this was the right fit. It also connected with my growing ideas aimed at re-discovering a role for the church with the people unlikely to connect with the evangelical version I grew up with. Ministering with people whom Jesus would connect with, but didn't fit traditional religion, sounded decidedly Biblical. Church planting was the key to this world. I was hooked.

I later learned it wasn't so much the allure of church planting that attracted me to my specific kind of ministry. Rather, it was the chance to live out my callings, (the Great Commandment, Great Commission, and a church that seeks to build the gifts of all of its members), to a world of nones and dones. My own "yes" moment wasn't when I became a church planter, passed an assessment, or started a service. It was the time, and many times since, I re-commited to love others and live out the fullness of my gifts with the people God's already working in too.

My story twists and turns from here but my calling to join the unfolding mission of God in my city, even when it took me beyond comfort and safety, hasn't wavered since. I planted my first church in 2009, and my second in 2016. (I'll share more about these church plants throughout the book.) I discovered my passion in ministry, the dreams and ideas in my head started to make sense, and when I responded to turn ideas real, they started to take flight.

Your Calling

Before we go further, don't hear that your idea is for *more* in a culture that overvalues busyness. Rather, consider it a calling into *deeper* with what you *already have*. Christians tend to miss the pieces God has *already* given when making or measuring decisions. We already have clear callings to inform our actions today and tomorrow. Our struggle is living them out. Our first step is often waiting for the perfect conditions and confirmation before taking the risk. What if this is backwards? What happens if our first step is to ensure our dream or idea fits one of the foundational callings, and our second immediate step is to try it out?

The callings as individuals to love one another, and the callings as church, combine to form clear direction. Yet we struggle to be transformed by them. Why is this? We've heard, "love thy neighbor," but loving the "other," the people who are the least like us, is hard. Why else do most churches look the same? Same skin color, same theology, same income bracket.

Part of our unwillingness to branch out and turn dreams real is the stark possibility of failure. Admittedly, it's normal to wait for the perfect moment or keep rechecking plans to ensure they're the best they can possibly be before launching a new idea. We'll discuss the culture of risk later, but what if we changed the measure? Calling has nothing to do with achievements. Rather it has everything to do with our faithful response of "yes" to the picture of better God has attached to our calling. The Bible is full of inspirational tales of heroes faithfully embarking on their adventure and crossing into an unknown world of trial, error, and victory. The greatest of these is about God. In the Garden, Adam and Eve make their choice and are banished, yet God crosses the threshold from the Garden to chase after the banished. God not only pursues but never appears to leave until the time after the Exile to Babylon. (God never leaves, it's just that to us, 400 years seems like an absence.) God is a defining part of unfolding history, from Noah to Abraham to Moses, to the Temple and the nation of Israel, and beyond. God crossed the threshold of the heavenly realm, dwelt among his creation, and now rules at the mercy seat of the altar. The remarkable acts of Jesus entering the world to usher in a grand new hope and rescue plan are not just for the chosen few, but the entire cosmos. As if the incarnation, death, and resurrection aren't shocking enough, you and your church are invited to participate uniquely as part of the rescue solution. God invites us to take part in the opportunity to glimpse heaven now, to let your unique dream for better unfold in space and place. But this only happens when we say "yes" to the call. The action to live out your dream for better makes all the difference, not its result. Will you say "yes" to start living out your picture for better in your world? A guarantee of success is not part of the plan and not your concern. Your measure is your faithfulness to stand and be accounted for. How will you proceed?

It's time to start turning dreams real, and the first step is to start testing what works and what doesn't. That's harder than it sounds.

In our digital and social media connected world generating empathy and compassion isn't hard. Anyone can freely offer thoughts and prayers to right systemic injustice. It's quite another scenario to move from, "let's do something about it," to "look at what we're *doing* about it." We need more of the latter. With your dream for better, be it for ministry, neighborhood, person or people, let's propel it forward.

Chapter 10

Opportunity Awaits

---

*"Impossible is just a big word thrown around by small men that find
it easier to live in the world they've been given than to explore the
power they have to change it. Impossible is not a fact. It's an opinion.
Impossible is not a declaration. It's a dare. Impossible is potential.
Impossible is temporary. Impossible is nothing."*

- Muhammad Ali

If you woke up tomorrow with a blank slate, a time and space where
you had no responsibilities or expectations, what would you do differently? Just like the lottery winnings, since we're not going to
wake up tomorrow in this illusion, what's stopping you from making small shifts or movements to make your idea, whatever the size,
real today? The time to make it happen is right now. Here's why.

Awakenings

The last mass church planting movement in the U.S. happened
during the great Awakenings at the turn of the 19th century. One
reason the movement tipped was pragmatic. A large percentage of
Americans were not part of any organized religious body. Evangeli-

calism filled the void and grew largely unabated until the start of the 20th century when fundamentalism emerged. Despite a slow down, growth continued until just after the Second World War. The rise of secularization, coupled with the slow exit started by baby boomers, slowed the proliferation of religiosity in North America. Today, few (if any) contemporary faith movements are growing exponentially, and it's due to similar reasons—most people were/are already churched. Christendom means a high saturation of Christian affiliation that hampers any exponential growth potential. However, as we've already learned, the market is shifting and a new opportunity is emerging.

In Canada, the French province of Quebec saw a sharp decline in religious affiliation in a matter of years. The radically successful "Quiet Revolution" was a period of cultural and political shifts that rejected heavy integration with the Roman Catholic Church in favor of secularism. In the fifty years since, Quebec looks more like France than Canada in terms of religious participation among its population. In 2015, I was in Montreal attending a church planting conference. This particular one was no different than any other including the usual celebrated planting methods and American celebrity headliner. Included in the event was the usual fanfare over successful church plants and their rapid rise to well-attended services. But there was one feature that struck me. It was the *kind* of church plant—in Quebec of all places—that was succeeding. A purely attractional model centered entirely on an exceptional service in a cool venue. It was a straight copy from the seeker sensitive era of the 1980s and 90s. Yet here it was, a seeker sensitive church reaping huge success in the least religious province in Canada. How did it happen?

Thankfully, the keynote speaker (which happened to be Ed

Stetzer) admonished the listeners that the successful plant was not reproducible; it was not something the average church could afford or replicate in their cultural context. We're in a cultural age where adding more churches doesn't address how the gospel message is received by outsiders. This church plant was successful because of a complete turnaround in religious affiliation. The model wasn't the key, even though it was being trumpeted as such. Religious affiliation in Quebec has been declining for decades, to the point the culture has gone *full circle*. A contemporary attractional church service was met with interest rather than disdain because the bad memories of the past church-dominated era had been forgotten in subsequent generations.

The model may not be one to replicate in your context, but it identifies a critical feature in North American culture. It doesn't take long to "forget" about religious roots. Maybe two or three generations (sociologists will have to confirm this). Quebec is a glimpse of what's unfolding in major metropolitan centers. Culture is shifting, without the church at the helm, and we can view our new position as either *opportunity* or *threat*. Those who see a threat looming on the horizon will batten down the church doors and refrain from venturing outside. Can they survive much longer? Many churches may not last another generation. Plus, if our calling is to live as full participants in God's unfolding kingdom, our activity should push us beyond self-service. The other option is to look at the culture and note a growing opportunity. In our culture we're waking to a potential blank slate.

White Space

Ori Brafman writes in his book *The Chaos Imperative* about methods to increase productivity and innovation in organizations. One of the three critical pieces to accommodate innovation is the concept of white space: *"a time or place or system unfettered by an established structure."*[34] It acts as the potential launching point to replace culture, systems, or institutions. A forest fire is nature's way of creating white space of new growth and potential. Brafman uses the example of the plague in the 12th century, and the widespread death of Roman Catholic clerics who controlled the dissemination of most knowledge and education, as white space for new learning spheres, including the rapid establishment of major universities across Europe.

White space is a blank slate to view the world in a different way (such as through a missional lens). New sights and sounds in a world where what was once impossible now seem faintly possible. *Post-Christendom is the white space for the church and your dream.* It is a moment of opportunity, not impediment. It's an opportunity because the kingdom is already unfolding in our new culture, with or without a participating church. It is opportunity because, although people may not know the gospel stories off-hand, they remain spiritual and tuned to what the kingdom narrative has to offer. Love, justice, beauty, and hope all have transcending appeal. In fact, post-Christian culture isn't necessarily anti-Christian and certainly isn't anti-Jesus. Religious nones may not claim affiliation, but are not by default antagonistic. Remember, only a small percentage of people claim to be atheists.[35] If anything, there's indifference for religion and a curiosity for faith. It's a population that's interested in things spiritual but suspicious of institutions. There has been a decline in church attendance but only a slight decrease in people who consider

---

[34] Brafman, *The Chaos Imperative*, 15.
[35] There is no atheist movement replacing the declining church. Consult Stark, *The Triumph of Christianity*, 374

themselves spiritual (measured in belief in higher power, in prayer, spiritual practices, etc.).[36] This implies that although most of our churches are poorly equipped to connect with the culture beyond the church walls, that culture continues to search for answers to meet their desires to be seen (by God). This certainly sounds like a profound opportunity. This is why the time to act is now.

We are in a white space moment. The disintegration of the institutional church is a *veiled opportunity*. It's time to try our new ideas to discover how they connect into God's kingdom hope today and for the future. Your dream fits into this white space reality, regardless of shape, form, or size. In fact, when your dream starts to take shape, you're literally starting a new cultural *movement*. Sound farfetched? It isn't. But in order to build one we need to have the right environment.

---

[36] You can consult a number of sociologists on this topic. Bibby and Thiessen are two in Canada.

Chapter 11

Culture Revolution

"Change, real change, is the result of focused persistence."
- Seth Godin

The church in the West suffers from a distinct lack of innovation. We already know institutions don't shift with ease. We want meaningful improvements, culture changes, and growth through evangelism but are withheld by a lack of capable leaders, rules and belief systems, and complacency. However, the institution isn't the only organization that can't handle change. There are countless examples of big companies who can't respond fast enough to capitalize on big threats or opportunities. When a business identifies a threat looming on the horizon often the change is too slow or the success in the present too distracting.

Kodak was the developer of the digital camera and had the opportunity to corner the market early. Instead, they chose to ignore the potential because it would disrupt the comfortable systems they had in place. Rather than change their interface, in a last ditched attempt to survive, Research In Motion (RIM) actually tried to persuade new iPhone users to return to Blackberry, offering the full cost of the iPhone as incentive. Blockbuster didn't think Netflix was a threat to the video rental business. Walt Disney Animation Studios insisted on "what's always worked" in storytelling and animation. Their ingrained culture couldn't produce a hit film for a decade, while innovative Pixar cranked out *Toy Story*, *Finding Nemo*, and *The Incredibles*.

I grew up in Western Canada, but I still recall the news stories coming out of the East Coast in 1992. The cod fishery, lifeblood for the industry in Eastern Canada, collapsed overnight. A hundred thousand jobs ground to a crushing halt, producing an economic blow that remains in the local economy today. The collapse, however, wasn't unexpected. Scientists had warned for years that the fish count was in trouble. Unfortunately, the short-sightedness of the industry and politicians contributed to the massive and demonstrable collapse. Nearly 25 years later only tiny sections of the Atlantic are showing any signs of recovery.

Size is often mistakenly equated with stability. This rhetoric is changing especially in the wake of the financial collapse in 2008. When the banking sector went down like a house of cards, a failure due to years of unscrupulous mortgage deals, only government intervention stemmed the losses. Other institutions are susceptible to the same collapse, such as the church. It is difficult for established institutional organizations, governments, and churches to make significant changes in short periods of time. It is possible through incrementalism—small changes implemented over long periods of time. The problem we face is the patience for timeframes that extend into generations. Instead, like the finance sector before collapse, we opt for the quick fix or short-term gain. Take your pick of the latest strategies from National Church Development, Seeker Sensitive, Purpose Driven, Emerging, Emergent, Church Planting,

Discipleship Making Movements, Multi-Site, the list goes on. We need deeper and lasting changes for both the institution and the nimble faith communities of the future. That will require change that goes beyond a shift of activities where we address inconsequential things like the music during the service, the content of the sermons, or youth programs. We must ask a core question related to mission: how can we lead culture shifts that embrace God's existing mission in order to survive today and thrive tomorrow?

Creating a culture that embraces *innovation* is a necessary instrument to lead effective change. Innovation is a form of planning for what's next. Institutions aren't very good at it. We need innovation to survive but most often lack the culture to accommodate it. However, despite an institutional environment that operates against innovation, mainstream culture is shifting to our advantage. Our technology dependent culture has been shaped by rapid shifts both in product adoption and communication methods. Even the constant change in platforms for the world's top social media brands helps prepare people to accept rhythms of innovation. For example, Facebook's billion users are used to changes to the interface. For a day or two people may be upset, but nobody closes their account over the loss of the "poke" button. With this potential advantage in mind, let's explore ways to disrupt the old with new.

Disruptive Technologies

In the manufacturing sector, innovation occurs in two ways: *sustaining* technologies or the embrace of *disruptive* technologies.[37] Sustaining technologies maintain status quo and incrementally improve production. Performance may increase along with the assurance of

---

[37] See Christensen, *The Innovator's Dilemma.*

reliability. This works so long as the factory delivers to known markets. On the other hand, disruptive technologies make short-term production *worse*. This type of innovation challenges established systems and ruins the status quo, all to create new systems that address emerging market trends. It's risky, but despite short-term loss, disruptive technologies are necessary because they respond to tomorrow's mainstream. Without disruptive technologies a manufacturer would continue producing old widgets *even when the market moves on*. In other words, death.

What are some of the disruptive technologies in our churches today? Perhaps a better initial question is, do we even have space for disruptive technologies? I remember when I went through the rounds of assessments to become an approved church planter with that large denomination. I passed all the tests, but because the model I had for "church" was too different from the big suburban culture, I was cut loose. Their culture had no frame of reference to understand, let alone support, my ideas for ministry. In fact, ten years later, the level of innovation in that denomination still hasn't changed much. They're interested in sustaining technologies.

Building a Culture of Innovation

Some companies aren't threatened by change. In fact it's necessary for their survival. Toy company Hasbro, for instance, constantly innovates to produce new exciting toys for each buying season. If they didn't, they'd lose market share every Christmas. The cellular divisions of Apple and Samsung must produce new versions of their best sellers or wind up like Microsoft and RIM. The latter were too slow to offer new products and eventually were squeezed out of the market. Between Kodak and Hasbro, RIM and Apple, or Blockbuster and Netflix, the difference between success and failure has a lot to do with their culture for innovation that permitted necessary disruption. How can you build this culture?

The first way is to start fresh with an environment built to anticipate and expect constant change. In a church context, spaces where a new culture can take shape would include church plants. When you can't start fresh, the alternative is to change existing culture. This approach is far more challenging since you have to win an appeal for people to change rather than attracting those who "get it" from the get-go. It's in many ways easier to start something brand new outside of the bounds of established organizational culture. It's not easy to change in environments where the status quo is guarded. In fact most established organizations, even ones with cultures for creativity and innovation, struggle with letting go of predictability. For churches that means on one hand, the ones that embrace new ideas risk alienating parishioners who just want the Goldilocks experience. On the other hand, churches that claim they're open to new ideas, but in reality deem newness unseemly, the parish grows frustrated. How should we move forward?

Accept More Risk

I know leaders who attend church planting or leadership conferences and get inspired, yet lament they can't apply new ideas back home. A middle-aged pastor with no transferable skills considering radical new direction for his church is taking a huge risk. He stands to lose more than just the vision from an idea. If a stagnant congregation can't handle change the Goldilocks conundrum may kick-in and disgruntled parishioners will leave for the church down the road. I have a pastor friend who lost 25% of his congregation when he implemented missional DNA (more on him later). The pragmatic concerns of budgets and expense sheets looms over crucial plans for what's next. Instead we settle for temporary or minute changes that wind up doing little to address root problems of individualism, consumerism, and discipleship. We need ways to accommodate innovation.

Ed Catmull, president of Pixar, describes the culture in one of the world's most innovative animation studios.[38] Building cultures that welcome innovation depends on the acceptance of risk that permits the evolution of new ideas. At Pixar, they know originality is fragile and deserves to be protected. Organizations must be intentional in protecting new ideas from being judged too quickly. Another key factor in culture building is ensuring new ideas are constantly being introduced into the system. An intentional rhythm to accept new ideas and people needs to be embraced widely.

Implementing these features to spearhead innovation and risk taking often depends on where you start. An organization that begins with a culture that expects change and innovation is easier to build. Trying to change an established institution is much harder. For most churches, there is a distinct lack of internal mechanisms designed to challenge the status quo from within. One could certainly argue the Holy Spirit is the innovative force breathing fresh life into rote traditions. But that would require listening and activating to the call of the Spirit. Often it doesn't matter where innovative ideas come from, change from within the institution remains difficult.

Increasing organizational risk and welcoming new ideas will consistently face oppositional forces bent on maintaining status quo. That's why in order to build rhythms of innovation, protection of ideas, and the eventual emergence of new expressions, a

---

[38] Read his book *Creativity, Inc.*

certain kind of leadership is needed. Leaders who will craft space for new dreams and propel necessary change forward need to be at the helm.

Lead Change

One of the seminal works on managing organizational change is John Kotter's book *Leading Change*. It's worth the pick up even though it's designed for the corporate world. Alan Hirsch and Michael Frost design church applications using Kotter's ideas in their book *The Faith of Leap*. When describing a church leading change, Frost and Hirsch remarked how noticeably different it looked compared to one merely managing its existence. A church that can shift culture is an "adventurous church [that] thrives on a sense of holy urgency."[39] *Adventure, urgency, thrive*—all words that sound like a church that's alive. The pragmatic question is, *how* can you usher in new innovative ideas into an immovable institution? The answer? You try a formula that's been used before. Luckily, innovation in church culture can take on a number of different shapes. There's no one-size-fits-all approach. That doesn't mean renewal from within is without difficulties, but it does open up the door to possibilities, including your ideas.

Ushering in new ideas is a challenge to existing paradigms and cultures. Most communities will try a strategic approach to increase the chances of change sticking. There are many strategies, designs, and formulas to choose from when it comes to church innovation. It could be Purpose Driven, or 3DM, or APEST, or V3, or Parish Model, or 5Q, or Slow Church, or Organic Church Movements, or DMM, or CPM, or 100 Movements, or 4 Square, or whatever. The

---

[39] Frost and Hirsch, *The Faith of Leap*, 41.

list goes on. How do you choose?

It's your job as leader, dreamer, or idea maker, to go through the exercise of distilling potential ways to turn ideas real successfully in your world. One basic process includes two steps. Step one is spending the time listening and articulating the need in your context and culture. This will ensure you don't fall into the trap of copying popularity over practicality (church exceptionalism). After that, operate like any good artist and steal what fits your community best. Take pieces from a variety of sources to create the best possible platform that gives new ideas and dreams the best chance to succeed and produce lasting shifts. From here culture begins to change as people discover how a new story of mission impacts their lives and those around them.

Chapter 12

Movements

---

*"If you cannot understand that there is something in man which
responds to the challenge of this mountain and goes out to meet it,
that the struggle is the struggle of life itself upward and forever
upward, then you won't see why we go."*
- George Mallory, Adventurer

*W*hen you start living out your dream, or the dream of the community, you are starting a movement. It's not a successful one yet, but it's the start of one. In church leadership culture, many are used to "movement language," be it disciple-making movements, church planting movements, or social justice movements. Despite movement rhetoric few church movements hit mass adoption in North America. Here's what I mean.

Bigger isn't Better
Whether it's Facebook, Twitter, or Pinterest, the social media age offers unique tools that can catalyze monumental change, or condone the non-participating yet vocal "slacktivist." The volume of content makes locating what's important in local, national, and international news exhausting and never-ending. Despite attempts to control the dissemination of "fake news," social media sites still function

in basically the same way. Ranking algorithms, determined by your preferences, will feature certain content, and the more popular content appears (based on user votes), the more likely you are to see it. When a particular topic reaches a certain threshold of views, it continues to snowball as more views and interactions determine value and importance, which translates to even more exposure and views (this ignores paid advertising used to increase prominence). The problem with the popularity system for media and user is twofold: bad ideas spread further faster, and our picture of success is defined through a lens of consumerism where *bigger is equated to better.*

For example, do you remember the maligned craze "Kony2012," launched by young Americans with good intentions but poor judgment and little experience? The campaign sought to find and prosecute Joseph Kony, leader of the malicious Ugandan guerrilla group the Lord's Resistance Army. The lucrative campaign took off at the beginning of March 2012, and in a matter of weeks generated so much online attention that it became the most successful nonprofit campaign ever in terms of online views, surpassing the likes of World Vision and their decades of TV sponsored programming. Yet despite hundreds of millions of views and just as many dollars, Joseph Kony is still hiding in the jungles of Uganda, and Invisible Children, the organization behind it all, faded from the spotlight almost as quickly as it appeared. The impact from all of the interest was nascent at best, but it did offer an important lesson: it exposed the vulnerability of churches to the allure of mass appeal. What captured our attention in Kony2012 wasn't the cause but the popularity. We blindly connect scale with substance because there's perceived safety and legitimacy in numbers, even if the purpose is untrue or unattainable.

The problem rests in our expectations of success, which in turn fuel a pressure to find answers. Most church leaders are readily aware of the slow decline in overall church participation. In response, many are turning to new strategies to kick-start revival in a new era. Starting movements is attractive because the results are attractive: being responsible for the next church movement that solves problem X, Y, or Z. It's good vision and strong motivation to set an ambitious dream just out of reach of the community's grasp, but when movement ideas have expectations of exponential growth and viral change, we develop momentum based on fleeting qualities rather than substantive ones. Our drive for scale chases strategic fads rather than substance.

Challenging Church Movement Language

Have you heard some of the exciting stories about church planting movements (CPM) and discipleship multiplying movements (DMM) from around the globe? Often missionary groups regale us with tales about house churches in India or China experiencing contagious growth in countries parched for Jesus. The desire in North America is to have the same results. Trouble is, the cultural conditions abroad are crucial factors to the descriptive factors of CPMs, which for the most part do not exist here. But this hasn't stopped the proliferation of CPM language here, and with it come grand expectations. David Garrison defines church planting movements as "a rapid multiplication of indigenous churches planting churches that sweeps through a people group or population segment."[40] Garrison clarifies he is merely describing movements already active in the mission field, not prescribing how to develop them. This is an important distinction, because leaders in North

---

[40] Garrison, Church *Planting Movements*, 2.

America may borrow language and features from Garrison's definition. Words like "rapid," "exponential," or "contagious" are used to
define the vision of a local church. We associate bigger and faster
with better (and healthier).

It's not only global missions informing our function. Perhaps
an even greater influence is the market economy. When the church
adopts terminology and strategies usually reserved for profit maxi-
mizing firms, we ironically limit our potential. Market place ideas
like "tipping the scales" or "exponential growth" produce a level
of undue expectations on potential church (or people) movements.
We can learn some lessons from the marketplace, but they must be
interpreted carefully so our values for people, transformation, and
sustainability trumps appeal and attendance. If not, the eventual
result will be the same problem social media campaigns face: the
belief that bigger is better, and once big is quickly achieved you'll
earn lasting impact. But scale is fleeting. Churches no longer receive
automatic relational equity with their neighborhoods. Relationships
have to be earned and that takes time. When we pursue the allure
of large multiplying movements, we develop our hopes within the
confines of expectations from the mission field or the free market,
coupled with timeframes borrowed from Christendom when altar
calls worked.

The hope of the church moving forward won't be found in the
mass appeal of the most popular churches. Rather, I believe it will
be the accumulation of many small movements, ones that may only
reach as far as neighborhood boundaries, that will renew our cities.
Movement language itself isn't bad. Rather, the solution to realize
more movements is the belief *small counts big.* Your idea, no matter
the size, counts. And in order for those ideas to live up to your
dream of better, they must tip into movement state. We must value

in practice that small collaborations are changing neighborhoods and people where traditional church expressions are not. With your dream in hand, let's explore building movements of a different kind.

Chapter 13

A New Definition for Church Movements

"Life is much more meaningful - and also much more fun - when you take charge and act."

- Srdja Popović

In 2011, the Arab Spring stoked a powerful wave of protest in Middle Eastern countries. Pictures of the revolution from Egypt in particular stick in my mind. The uprising was monitored by a passive military, including attack helicopters hovering over the crowds, their menacing presence undone by constant green laser beams from people below. North Americans saw the tail end of the revolution once media coverage sent pictures to the world. But did you know the revolution was years in the making?

Before 2011, a small group of Egyptians gathered in a nondescript Mediterranean hotel. This wasn't a vacation, however, but a secret learning event. The topic: how to start and sustain a nonviolent movement. The facilitators? Leaders from the successful people movement Otpor!, the group instrumental in the eventual collapse of Serbian President Slobodan Milošević.[41] Although the mass of Egyptians crowding Tahrir Square for days, weeks, months on end, wasn't guaranteed, the planning that led to the final months was heavily orchestrated by a few. The Egyptian Revolution overthrew the president and ushered in an age of change (and uncertainty). Why did it work? What made the Egyptian movement different from the comparatively successful movement in Tunisia, the initial success in Yemen, and unlike the humanitarian crisis that emerged in Syria?

Successful movements balance between intentional planning and organic growth. They can be planned, but only to a certain extent, because movements, particularly ones that revolve around people like social or church movements, are unpredictable. For this reason it's useful to approach movements with a working definition that's wide enough to accommodate spontaneous change, concise enough to clearly motivate people towards a particular purpose, and characterized so even small movements are regarded as important achievements.

We begin with some questions. Do movements need to hit a certain size before they become movements? Do they require growth by multiplication before they count? Are they measured in impact? Or by how long they last? The answer: none of the above.

All movements, be they product-driven or social, need people. Getting people together to surround an idea, dream, or problem requires empathy.[42] A new cause needs people who care and understand what's at stake. With that in mind, here's a simple starting definition we will build from:

---

[41] Popović, *Blueprint for Revolution*, 2015.
[42] Feldmann, *Social Movements for Good*, Chapter 2.

Movement is a group action.

Orchestral compositions usually have self-contained parts called "movements." I regularly attend my local philharmonic orchestra, and one evening a rambunctious concerto by Sergei Rachmaninoff awaited. Rachmaninoff has written some of the greatest piano concertos in the classical repertoire, with a distinct bold and intense style that features the full breadth of the piano's range. Search for Piano Concerto No. 2 in C minor, Op. 18, and listen to the powerful solo melodies you may be familiar with. The listeners that evening were enthralled. The loud crashing bangs and brisk tempo ultimately culminated in a rapturous climactic end much to the delight of the standing crowd who gave three ovations. The amount of coordination required by each individual player coupled with the directions from the conductor is staggering. The result is an expression of music in its highest form.

Movements are *coordinated* group action.

The Occupy movement took off at the pit of the Great Recession in the fall of September 2011. The motto was clear: "we are the 99%." The so-called masses were calling for wealth redistribution, pitting the richest 1% against the remaining 99%. How to achieve that goal was utterly unclear. Occupy was a collection of various organizations and individuals all with different ideas (assuming they had ideas at all). Coming off the heels of Arab Spring, the Occupy movement picked up rare momentum across North America, and for a brief moment a social movement claiming to include the 99% looked like it might tip that way. If it had, substantial change could have swept across the continent, grinding the status quo, and the free market, to a halt. But it didn't. Status quo is hard to beat, especially when you lack a shared plan.

Momentum stalled because, as a whole, there was no consensus on how to address the systemic problems of wealth distribution. Without a united cause, gathering groups are just that—mere gatherings—like fans cheering a sports team. Temporarily coordinated but lacks a specific *cause*. The Occupy movement became its own pariah and failed because it not only lacked coordination, but more importantly, lacked a common shared purpose that could fuse fragmented groups. Shared purpose provides clarity of purpose that acts as a foundation to build needed momentum.

Mass social movements seem to be gaining popularity in the West. Compared to Occupy, the Black Lives Matter (BLM) movement has found more success. Although they are decentralized in chapters, they still share common structures and organizational goals. This has helped maintain a common direction and clarity for onlookers. The Women's Marches throughout North America have produced incredible turnouts. The #metoo movement, which after ten years, tipped into movement state with the help of social media. It highlights violence against women, particularly sexual assault, and pushes for significant cultural changes. #NeverAgain, after yet another deadly high school shooting, is gaining momentum across America, built to challenge the sick idolization of gun culture. Will these movements yield lasting change? Or will they fizzle out like Occupy? #metoo has already made a significant cultural impact. And although the extent of change is difficult to measure in the present, from BLM to Women's March to Never Again, all have a chance to change the course of history. What they require as they go, however, is maintaining absolute clarity on purpose. *What* are they trying to achieve together? Once that's set, the *how* it can happen unravels.

Movements are coordinated group action towards *shared purpose*.

Take note, this definition makes no mention of numbers. I wish to suggest that there is no multiplying threshold that must be met in order to qualify a legitimate movement.[43] Rather, it is unifying people into coordinated action towards a shared cause that counts. This can include a variety of expressions, timeframes, and sizes. When coordinated action exists towards a shared cause, you're on the move, and are a movement. Two or three neighbors advocating for a change in a bus route counts as a movement, albeit a small and temporary one, but a movement nonetheless.

Movements could include a few church small groups united towards a cause of injustice. It not only counts, but should be celebrated as well. Those groups *could* expand to incorporate the entire congregation and beyond, but it was a movement prior to increasing size. When we incorporate exponential factors of growth to movement language we underestimate and discredit the activity of the bold few. Today's church should seek out every inspiration and activity to champion. This does not imply growth should not be an attribute to successful movements. Lofty goals may require the mobilization of the multitude to become effective. But when it comes to the re-invented church, mass appeal isn't the goal, the accumulated impact of many ideas in motion is.

Before the final definition on movements, a note of caution. Merely gathering, even in large groups, does not make a movement. Action towards a cause that's sustained long enough to meet a goal

---

[43] There's certainly a correlation between the size of a movement and the size of the problem. Changes to your cultural norms versus changes to neighborhood will require more people to adopt the cause. I'm suggesting that movements can occur for smaller issues with fewer people, something you're likely to encounter more often in the context of community.

is. Movements enact change and inspire people to call a particular idea or dream their own. Leaders should understand that a successful imparting of a particular vision works when people start calling that vision their own. Ownership is critical to generating momentum and sustainability. How to get there is the next step.

Definition: **Movements are coordinated group action towards shared purpose** *that enacts lasting change.*

Chapter 14

Movements That Last

"Revolution is the new status quo." - Sally Hogshead

Now that we've developed a definition for movements, the next question is: how do we build and sustain one? Return to your dream for better and apply it as the central cause in the definition of movement. From here we need to build necessary longevity so we can give the dream a chance to meet its final goal.

How To Start a Movement That Lasts

We begin with some theory on adoption rates in movement theory. Here's a quick overview of a graph many are familiar with, called the adoption curve or diffusion of innovation curve.

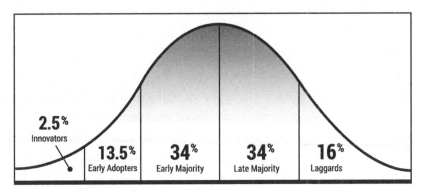

This graph depicts different people in our communities, and ways to compel them to join an idea or vision. Starting on the far left are the Innovators. Innovators are the apostles and sometimes prophets in our churches. They are the dreamers who put out new ideas first. Few people are constantly disrupting status quo like Innovators. They challenge assumptions and intentionally try to break systems. Anybody can dream for better, but Innovators routinely try to turn dreams real. Although they are perennial starters, they usually can't sustain movements on their own. A single Innovator struggles to make lasting impact because her success is reliant on being legitimized by a participating majority. The secret to kickstarting movements is getting Innovators to convince the majority of people to believe in a dream.

Belief starts to arrive when the Early Adopters enter to participate. Here are people who generally accept risk and embrace change. The Early Adopters may not be self-starters, but they come alongside new ideas quickly even when they do not completely understand them. If Innovators and the Early Adopters gathered and coordinated activity towards shared purpose they would be a movement, however, they would lack large scale impact and longevity (Innovators tend to bore quickly).

Gathering the Innovators and the Early Adopters is easy compared to the majority. These segments are the people who "get it" without much explanation. It would include the church planter and the sending team. Including more people in the dream is the hard part. At this point, significant forces will grind your potential to a halt. Leaders may know from experience there's a point where a new idea either tips into adoption by the majority or stalls out as a crazy idea before eventually dying. In order to break this resistance there needs to be a way to compel the next segment of people, the

Early Majority, to participate. How can we do this? We turn to the tech industry and a "make or break" moment found in product adoption for answers.

A theory introduced in the 1980s by Geoffrey Moore, in a book entitled *Crossing the Chasm,* describes product adoption along our curve. New products face the same challenge as new ideas. Making the leap from forgotten gadget to mass adoption relies on one thing: compel the majority of people to jump on board. A key to growing movements so they reach their goal and desired impact depends on inspiring the majority of people in your community to adopt the dream. The problem? The Early Adopters and Early Majority think and live so differently Moore separates them with what he calls "the chasm."

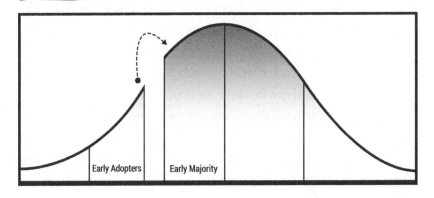

Want to create the next killer product? Start a movement that enacts lasting change? Your success lies in crossing this chasm. To illustrate this concept think about a tablet computer. The iPad wasn't the first tablet to hit the market, but it's certainly the most successful. Starting in the early 1990s the first commercial tablets emerged. You probably don't recall the Apple Newton personal digital assistant because very few sold. You might remember Palm

Pilots—they had a brief tenure as the next big tech gadget, but they faded away after a few short years. The realm of tablet computing went silent until 2010, when on the back of the successful iPhone, Apple prepped the launch of the iPad. They conducted exceptional market analysis and knew that Apple enthusiasts could be relied upon to purchase new products (the Early Adopters), but they represented only a fraction of the potential market. Apple also knew the Early Majority and Late Majority were normal people simply looking for practical functionality in their devices. At the time heavy laptops were the mainstay for basic computing applications. The lighter iPad could be a monumental hit if Apple could prove to the Early Majority and Late Majority two crucial features: the tablet could check email, and surf the web. It sounds too simple, but once the majority of people caught wind that the iPad was an easier and lighter alternative to their laptops the scales tipped and consumers bought into the tablet craze. Apple made billions in revenue because it managed to "cross the chasm" by taking a new idea and translating it beyond the loyalists to the masses.

Now let's come back down to earth. It's unlikely billions in revenue is your goal. The social diffusion curve is usually used for mass adoption rates, but remember, movements don't require mass adoption. They do require groups of people, but that could be just a hundred or so in your church community. However, the same principles can apply because as a whole your community reflects the same broad division of adoption rates. The majority of people are tentative when approached with new ideas and need convincing.

Raising Ownership with Empathy

When ideas emerge in the community, how you share it will be crucial. Leaders cannot assume a whole congregation will resonate with a new vision in the same way. Getting Innovators and the Early Adopters on board with new ideas may be easy. Yet the power and longevity of a movement is reliant on convincing the majority of people, not just the Innovators, that the new will make pragmatic sense. Be it Egypt, the Maldives, or Serbia, all of these nonviolent movements would have amounted to little if the dreams of the average person were not a key appeal. The vision of the revolutionaries (the small segment of Innovators) is not enough to compel the body into any lasting change. Rather, it's necessary to empathize with the primary needs of the majority in your community, the empathy appeal, and speak to the average person offering the "why" a dream for better will make sense to them. Most people want a safe and familiar world and are uncomfortable with change. They, and will watch from the sidelines until they decide, "I could do that," or "That's important to me."

Every leader would love to see others care about their dream as much as they do. When this adoption shift happens, people on the sideline move from viewer to participant and *owner of a vision*. For example, you can mobilize people to stay interested in a particular outreach event, but it's quite another to develop longevity to address systemic problems in the city. For the iPad it's all of the Apple nerds who are brand evangelists. For the church, it's the people not merely excited for new vision, but they have adopted the new ideas as their own because they see themselves as part owner in the unfolding hope presented. That's a strong characteristic to have in any building movement but that chasm is in the way. What's the solution to jump the "chasm" and compel more owners to share the same dream? The answer is discipleship.

Chapter 15

Discipleship

"Discipleship is a way to curate your heart,
to be attentive to and intentional about what you love."
- James K.A. Smith, *You Are What You Love*

One weakness in most of our churches, but unequivocally the solution to reinvigorating sustained movements, is discipleship. Yet
challenges remain in the contemporary church. Countless churches
place significant value on discipleship, but struggle to produce disciples who disciple others. Part of the problem is that the relational
core of discipleship has been programmed. What was a two-year
meandering of life-on-life with Jesus has turned into a 12-week
Sunday school course. We've treated discipleship as a head exercise in learning the right ways of thinking, but have fallen short of
showing people the right way of living. Maybe it's because you and
I haven't been discipled well to begin with. Teaching is important,
but it's only a small component of the whole gospel experience.
For that we need to dig deep into the reality and muck of intense
relationships.

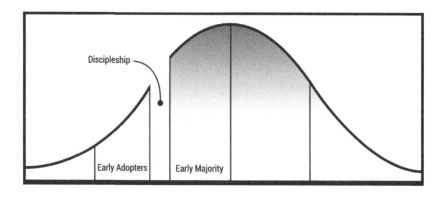

Product adoption requires some mechanism to prove to the majority that the new is safe and worth the change. The equivalent process in church community is formation centered around discipleship. It is the bridge between the early adopters and the majority. If discipleship can make or break a dream, vision, or movement, why is reproducible discipleship elusive? The church is tasked to chase a movement of disciple making. It is a unique pursuit to live lives that embody the character of Jesus. Discipleship challenges the core of inherited cultural assumptions, and for the church in the West, that includes rugged consumerism and individualism. These cultural features are in direct conflict with Christ-like discipleship. The church or community is challenged with the Goldilocks conundrum from Chapter 5. It's easier to hold weekly services than it is to challenge each and every person to seek depth rather than casual religious experiences. This is one of the reasons why producing a discipleship culture in your community is so hard. Although it would take a whole book to discuss this topic alone, I have two thoughts that explain why.

First, discipleship that reproduces other disciples is one of the weakest components in churches because Christ-followers are counter-cultural. Denying ourselves and picking up our cross daily works against the notion that our dreams and gifts are for ourselves. Our purpose in life isn't merely to achieve personal goals like better careers or bigger bank accounts. Second, discipleship should reflect the depth of the incarnation, and that includes a pursuit of our whole selves—mind, body, and soul. Traditional churches have long appealed to the mind (right thinking) delivered through a classroom. We struggle to appeal to the other senses. We also lack the patience to disciple, hoping to achieve in a few classes what may take *years* in life-on-life formation. Are you interested in discipleship at this pace and level of buy-in? We certainly need to mobilize more disciples if we're going to build movements, let alone exponential ones.

In my own life, I'm interested in helping people discover the fullness of their calling. I'm curious to coach people to turn their dreams into reality. To dream of better is a human attribute, and the journey to discover the fullness of our humanity is what ultimately fulfils us. When someone discovers the source that makes us full is the gospel, they can't help but respond and compel others to the same. In the midst of your plans and strategies, dreams and visions, start with people first. Love them, disciple them, and move forward together. Once this happens you have a greater chance to see a movement that lasts.

Chapter 16

SpiderFish

"To initiate change is to live out hope." - Unknown

*F*rodo and the hobbits had barely left the Shire before they encountered a mysterious ally—the Ranger of the North looming in the shadows of the human village pub. Once word had travelled about their perilous journey, unlikely alliances started to form. Even an elf and a dwarf, sworn enemies, joined the growing cadre. The quest spanned the known world where friends and foes crossed their paths. Ideas on how to overcome obstacles, impediments, and monsters emerged too. Although the destruction of the One Ring came down to the chosen few, it was the unique skills of The Fellowship that ultimately contributed to the success of the quest.

Creating a movement is a sizeable objective that looks good in theory, but along with developing culture to support innovation, it takes intention to generate an environment that can facilitate the best possible chance for success. The institutional church suffers from an inability to implement change in time to save itself. Yet at the same time I believe the hope to thrive in post-Christendom not only includes, but also relies on, that same church. We can preserve the value of institution while simultaneously generating space for new ideas to flourish. Here's one model to consider.

Starfish and Spiders

Ori Brafman and Rod Beckstrom wrote a seminal work on organizational development entitled *The Starfish and the Spider*. It didn't take long before innovators took the same concepts and applied them to church development. To summarize, organizations are classified in two broad categories: Starfish or Spiders. Spiders are traditional top-down organizations, built on hierarchy, where direction, culture, and control are handled by the few executives at the top. Most churches are centralized in this fashion. Spider organizations can benefit from strength in numbers and resources. They also are effective at sending messages top down. Their weaknesses are both survival and replication. Much like a spider, when the top (the head) fails, the entire organism shuts down. When the executives at RIM, Kodak, or Blockbuster, and maybe the contemporary church, failed to notice crippling market shifts in time, their mistake cost the entire business its existence. Despite the necessity of it, facilitating change in spider organizations is hard. The lack of freedom for decision making, and therefore innovation, contributes to an engrained culture that's hard to shift. They also have difficulty growing because only a few have the capacity to create and run another organization, while the rest watch or support. When growth happens, spiders can only replicate by addition—one spider at a time.

Starfish organizations are different. When starfish lose appendages the organism will not only survive, but each piece of a starfish has the DNA to produce *another* independent starfish. Starfish churches bear the belief of the priesthood of all believers in practice. They assume all Christians are capable of living out mission in their context. To accommodate this belief, power and decision making are decentralized, and the organization becomes nimble to change. However, there are problems with the starfish model including longevity. Can it survive long enough to pass along the replicating identity to enough people to spring a movement? Small and decentralized also has difficulty mobilizing towards large shared causes because of their size and independence.

The allure of starfish organizations in the church is the possibility of releasing more people to embody and join God's already unfolding mission and reverse church decline. Starfish organization looks similar to the decentralized early church operating in Asia Minor. But can we copy their success? Although some concepts of starfish organizations fit into contemporary church models, such as the priesthood of all believers, the practices currently don't match. Mobilizing the priesthood of all believers challenges the power of spider organizations—the head. Re-organizing from spider organization towards starfish challenges long-held and sensitive power structures. Many churches, and even new church plants, are not built to share power. We restrict who qualifies to fully represent the mission on behalf of the church.[44] The current leadership structures of spider organization are not replicating to offset the losses. We serve the needs of the internal community well but struggle to connect with the active kingdom beyond Christian borders. To put it in business terminology, spider churches building spider churches isn't scalable. What is scalable is disciples making disciples. What can we do to increase the number of disciples? We need to launch more starfish expressions. But how?

SpiderFish
Here's a pragmatic suggestion that accommodates needed innova-

---

[44] I don't think a church leader would tell someone they *aren't* qualified to participate on mission. I'm just saying ideas that take off under the official banner of the church tend to require approval (a method of control).

tion within the context of the institutional church without dismantling it. Starfish and spider organizations create an appearance that
they operate exclusive from each other. But what would happen if
we *combine* the two models? When I think about the possibilities of
church innovation, building diametrically opposed organizations is
counterproductive. Spider organizations (the institutional church)
are not disappearing, in fact, the largest ones are only getting larger
(at the expense of smaller ones). Conversely, starfish organizations
are not necessarily thriving (the parish church or house church
models lack resources, minus a few exceptional examples). What if
we looked at both organizations and leveraged the positives against
the negatives of each? This collaboration produces a new model:
SpiderFish.

I believe the church must address its decline in pragmatic ways.
That means retaining what works regardless of whether it comes
from the margins or the center of the institution. Both have pros
and cons worth keeping and discarding.

SPIDERS - The Institutional Church

Pros:

- Usually well resourced albeit those resources are declining.
- Hold tangible assets (like buildings).
- Have the most number of people in the pews.
- Have expertise and experience.

Cons:

- Centralized leadership.
- Threat of appeasing consumer Christianity.
- Lack innovative cultures.

- Build sustainability and safety.
- Change through slow incrementalism.
- Require Christendom to function best.

STARFISH - New Expressions and Ideas
Pros:
- Decentralized leadership with participating base.
- Created to handle and respond to change.
- Reflect culture of innovation and mission.
- Possibility of faster replication.
- Pioneering working kingdom expressions in post-Christendom.
- Reach outsider culture segments.
- Tend to be place or sub-culture specific.

Cons:
- Lack sustainability and longevity.
- Often lack critical mass of people to solve complex problems.
- Require significant commitments.
- Lack administrative expertise.
- Tend to be place or sub-culture specific.

SpiderFish organizations use the strengths of both to address the weaknesses in the other. A framework to generate new opportunities and longevity in a post-Christian age is the result. The two need to work together, not apart, because what one has the other lacks. For example, new church expressions need resourcing and support, namely money and people. The institution is not designed to deal with change, let alone innovation. The best they can hope for is what they're getting—incrementalism. In the meantime, we need to figure out a method to release *more* pioneers for the sake of mission. The current framework in spider churches isn't accomplishing this. SpiderFish ones can.

The Benefits of SpiderFish

- Permits the institution to change incrementally while simultaneously supporting needed innovation outside of institutional culture.
- Offers possibilities of sustainability to smaller kingdom expressions.
- The new expressions and pioneers provide necessary feedback to the institution on what works and what does not. This informs the incremental culture shifts.
- Enables multiple and responsive (faster) expressions to hit the ground running.
- Leverages the existing "bright spots" within the local body.
- Eliminates the threat of new ideas to the establishment by maintaining some control and distance.

Supporting new expressions that are connected to the established church is part of the SpiderFish model. It is a pragmatic solution that won't require dismantling the institution to produce results. However, that doesn't mean the institution doesn't have to undergo its own paradigm shifts, it just buys itself time to facilitate incremental change. Many industries, such as the energy sector, prominent in my home province, are implementing widespread organizational shifts to facilitate the need for nimble business models now deemed necessary to survive and profit in the new economic climate.[45] Major corporations like Exxon or Shell can't change their entire corporate structure overnight. However, smaller corporations can build the capacity to shift their function, assuming the leadership is willing to follow through with the necessary changes. The SpiderFish organization seeks to collaborate *between* large and small. In business terminology it's the large corporation launching a new division for research and development or a brand new venture. A new division benefits from the security of the big, while operating outside of rigid cultural expectations that may detract from thriving in a new environment.

What SpiderFish is not, however, is a temporary solution to address culture shifts. In his book "Accelerate", John Kotter presents a strategic model for hierarchical organizations called, "Dual System's Structure".[46] He addresses the struggle enterprises face with either avoiding looming market threats, or capitalizing on opportunities. To facilitate the innovation required to respond to both, the Dual System Structure retains the systems of organizational hierarchy while simultaneously creating a temporary network that operates in parallel. It sounds like a spider creating a starfish to work in tandem. Here's the difference. I'm not proposing a temporary solution that's designed to cease operations once a short-term objective is complete (e.g. planting a church). I'm advocating for the consistent testing and re-testing of new initiatives for the purpose of finding sustainable ones, and over the long-run potential autonomous bodies.

As a whole the church needs ways to create not mere movement,

---

[45] This article provides an example of the SpiderFish concept at work in the energy industry. Christopher Handscomb, Scott Sharabura, and Jannik Woxholth, "The Oil and Gas Organization of the Future," *McKinsey & Company*, September 2016, https://www.mckinsey.com/industries/oil-and-gas/our-insights/the-oil-and-gas-organization-of-the-future/.

[46] John P. Kotter, "*Accelerate: Building Strategic Agility for a Faster-Moving World.*" Boston: Harvard Business Review Press, 2014.

but *many* new movements. We don't need to rely on the hope of one new expression reaching mega church status. Rather, it's the accumulation of multiple implementers in the community, that when combined, reveal a movement state. In order to develop this initiative the institution must begin allocating more resources towards new and different ventures. Not merely more church planting, but forms of church planting we're unfamiliar with too.

The institution may have the resources and expertise to bankroll these new initiatives, but it's also not the only source. If we're looking at innovation, then it bears noting the new innovative ways to find funding. The emergence of social entrepreneurship and foundation grants are two that will play a role in future development of new kingdom expressions. Nonetheless, although institutions are facing declining pressures, they are the primary agent to respond to current opportunities in the short-run. We need more denominations and institutions willing to try more new things.

Where does the institution begin to look for new opportunities? Some already have their missions budgets at work, but as I noted earlier, we've treated mission as the ministry we do somewhere else, not here. The missional movement is a response to the mission we realize now to be right here in our own neighborhoods and cities. New opportunities exist right in our own backyard.

Your dream for better relies on the growing momentum of people sharing a cause and tipping into an effective movement. If you're in leadership you also want to develop others to live out their own journey and dreams in the same movement space as well. SpiderFish provides a potential template that combines small and innovative with the larger and established. But how do we find the pioneers to begin with? One way is find who's already working in your community without permission. They are the ones living out the subversive gospel in their space and place. We need to look for the *bright spots.*

Bright Spots

You may have heard about Jerry Sternin and his work in the 1990s with Save the Children, an international organization focused on delivering health, protection, and education to children. Looking to open an office in Vietnam, the government gave him six months to demonstrate measurable value before allowing his organization to settle. The issue he was required to address—child malnutrition—had no quick fix. The predominant strategies at the time could not produce results within his time constraints. He would have to try something new and innovative. Sternin overlooked the magnitude of the systemic issue and instead focused on what was actually working on the ground.[47] His search revealed a bright spot, a segment of children who had higher nutrition rates than their peers. His observations revealed subtle diet additions using readily available sources that made a significant difference. He took the findings and applied some basic principles to encourage others to replicate the same. The result was a measurable impact in a complex problem, made in a relatively short time. The bright spot was a win for Sternin, and it's the kind of win your church should be on the look out for too.

One tactic I encourage leaders to try is seeking out the innovators in their midst. There are untapped leaders already living out their ideas. Find these people, discover their talents, and legitimize their work by investing in those ideas *already at work.* Discovering these bright spots also reduces the leader's work. In essence it's a

---

[47] In behavior science this is called *positive deviance.*

form of "cheating." People who are bright spots have already done environmental analysis, already have the relationships, and are already operating as the hands and feet of the church on mission. All they may need is some level of investment and support. The payoff is worth it.

A SpiderFish culture is not threatened by new ideas from within the church for the sake of mission beyond. New ideas (initially) don't challenge the status quo. The benefits also include an accumulation of multiple ideas at work, which, when analyzed, inform the whole for larger strategic direction. It also encourages more people in our communities to live out their gifts and potential. This pursuit does, however, require accommodation. The discovery and building of bright spots needs designed space in the organization for people to try new ideas. That's why it's important to not only release the people living out God's mission in their world, but to build into them and tell their stories in the broader community as well. Doing so will generate momentum and compel others to live out their ideas. Not doing so will stymie the production of new ideas and much needed insight for the institution to survive. In a post-Christian context we need to embark on the mission beyond the church walls rather than restrict it. SpiderFish organization grants us the space to accomplish this goal.

Chapter 17

Presence

"I'll fly away, fly away, Oh Glory I'll fly away;
When I die, Hallelujah, by and by, I'll fly away."
- Albert Brumley

The old spiritual "I'll Fly Away" is a well known tune, but fails in theology. The chorus implies our place on earth has little value. It's heaven in the clouds we long for. This eschatology, popularized in the modern era, purports the extent of God's hope is to extricate chosen people into the heavenly realm. However, the orthodox Christian hope is something much different. It rests not in fleeing this world, rather, in "thy kingdom come, on earth as it is in heaven." God's promise is an age where New Heaven and New Earth collide in a restored universe. What we have in the here and now will be renewed. In many ways it's a fantastic promise that makes the mere notion of eternity in "heaven" seem plain. Heaven as our ultimate destination[48] is an unfortunate piece of modern Protestant eschatology that's led to the devaluation of something we need to

---

[48] I recommend reading N.T. Wright's book, *Surprised by Hope*, for a wonderful exploration of the Christian hope.

revitalize in a post-Christian world—presence.

A re-orientation towards the *missio Dei* must be accompanied with practices that revalue presence. Presence is part of the fundamental Christian identity because of our source—the incarnate Christ. The incarnation is about a God who chose to be present among humanity. Jesus fully immersed himself into the human experience through touch, smells, sights, sounds, triumphs, and hurts. Our God therefore is a contextual God who cares to dwell among us, know our names, and call us friends. In turn, as the Father sent the Son, we too are sent to reflect the character of Jesus in the places and spaces we dwell. That means living out the Great Commission and Great Commandment in church community, but into our neighborhoods and networks as well. It's the practice of loving our literal neighbors, and if you don't, the prayerful journey to get there.

One way to rediscover neighborhoods is the re-emergence of the parish model of church.[49] The parish idea of church community relies on the centrality of place. It seeks to recognize the kingdom at work in the immediate proximity, and develops church community to be alert and respond to local needs first. This often means teaching the church to discover and cultivate deep connections with their neighbors while encouraging them to live *in* rather than commute *to* the neighborhood. Valuing place means valuing the people in those places while rediscovering the mission out of our own homes. As the church discovers its place in the neighborhood, it simultaneously discovers that incarnate presence cannot be replicated by running a ministry or program through the church building. Rather, the

---

[49] One such movement is the Parish Collective based in Seattle, WA. Read, *New Parish* by Sparks, Friesen, and Sorens.

church serves where they live.

Bear in mind, the Great Commission reflects incarnate presence in discipleship with the one, but also stretches into the four corners of the world. Churches that develop an identity around place can *overvalue* location at the expense of other needs beyond the neighborhood. Exclusivity isn't the goal. We don't want to create community that ignores common realities. For example, many do not live and work in the same neighborhood. For this reason, I chase *presence* over *place*. Presence retains the elements of incarnation and value of local neighborhood, but includes where you're connected relationally even if it's not where you live. These all count as spaces to live out the *one* choice, *one* act, *one* moment in time to preview the kingdom in the here and now.

Commuter

Dallas, Texas, is one of those cities where you need a car to get around. I rented one while attending a missional church conference. Ten minutes after leaving the airport I was lost. I was looking for the freeway, and when I found one it happened to be *a* freeway not *the* freeway. I had never experienced, therefore could not expect, that *two* major freeways could be situated so close together. I was unfamiliar with the magnitude of Texan car culture.

My hometown is Calgary, Alberta, located on the Canadian Prairies at the foot of the Rocky Mountains. Our city has been designed intentionally as one big footprint (similar to LA, with a fraction of the population). All of our suburbs run one into the other from north to south, and east to west. Some large cities may count smaller counties or towns as part of their population; we have one big landmass, connected by roads upon roads, houses upon houses. If you want to travel anywhere outside of the downtown core you'll need a car. It's unlike major metropolitan cities where density is higher and walking is a cultural value. Most cities in North America overvalue space and unwittingly devalue proximity in the process. We overlook the power of place while attempting to legitimize commuter culture. Nonetheless, it's rare to encounter someone who, when given the choice, would choose a two-hour daily commute over a twenty-minute walk home. Calculate your own commuting time. The final tally may be *years* over a career spent in a car commuting. Is it worth the time?

Commuting has been normalized which means many of our churches are now commuter-oriented. In a conversation with a pastor from one of the largest evangelical churches in my city, I challenged central meeting spaces that extracted people from their neighborhoods into warehouse buildings in the middle of industrial parks or country fields. He argued getting people to drive to the central meeting place was a *strength* indicator! He also didn't believe that building small groups around geography was important. To him, driving 25 minutes to a small group was a demonstration of a deep commitment. He's not necessarily wrong, but his assumptions contribute to the continued devaluation of local neighborhoods. I contend extracting Christians from their communities has a *negative* impact on our overall witness. If on one hand you admonish your congregants to "love thy neighbor" yet conversely emphasize the need to gather in small groups (regardless of location) and come to a church service away from your neighbor, that church is sending mixed messages.

Going Postal

Unlike the pastor of the megachurch who thought driving 25 minutes was a value, there is growing interest in neighborhood revitalization (my story on JJ's Pub later) as people respond to invitations to connect with their community. For starters, we should work hard to intentionally connect people based on proximity to one another. Churches of any size can mobilize their small groups based on geography. Let's model in our churches that proximity is a value.

That same mega church years later hired a new pastor and something different is happening. Rather than hiring a small group pastor to train leaders so the leaders can go and do likewise in their small groups, this church is trying something different. They're organizing people based on postal (zip) codes. They still train small group leaders, but they're emphasizing the value of presence too. The results are outstanding: revitalized small groups, transformation in the neighborhoods, and the church reaching beyond the confines of the building to repair and restore the city streets where they dwell.

If we can fly away from this place to heaven in the sky, it's easier to treat our faith as mere religious insurance policies to cover our behavior and actions in this life. "God helps those who help themselves" becomes the mantra, vilifying the less fortunate and absolving the powerful from righting systemic problems. Conversely, if what's here will be rescued and restored, then we have a vested interest to do something about it. Not a return to grandma's church that sat at the center of culture, but a response to treat our homes as beacons of hospitality in our neighborhoods and beyond. Homes that reflect the power of presence and shared purpose acting in God's unfolding hope to restore the city.

Chapter 18

Collaborate

"Anyone who is not against you is for you." - Luke 9:50 (NLT)

*I*n the next two chapters I will share ideas on rethinking collaboration. You may be surprised to discover that as you re-orient towards a local presence worldview your ideas for better are shared by people outside of the church. Find who's already living it out and join the fray. You may not have to go far to find them.

Local Gems

There's a pub in my neighborhood called JJ's. It's a hole in the wall. Emphasis on hole. The running joke between my neighbor and me was to one day walk over and have a pint at JJ's. It was a full year before the veiled threats produced meaningful action. One late evening, sitting around a fire, we decided enough talk, we're going to JJ's. So off we went laughing about the stereotypes we were sure to encounter. As we turned the corner my smile dropped. Lined outside the pub were rows of bicycles. That's odd, JJ's looks *busy*. We stepped inside and found the only two available seats at the bar. What on earth is happening here? Turns out, the pub is usually busy on the weekend (they have their faithful clientele who frequent the proverbial neighborhood pub where everybody knows your name).

This particular night featured a once a month gathering for men in the neighborhood. It happened that an old high school friend of mine was among the crowd. Oh good, I thought, he'll give me some answers. When we started talking he didn't hesitate to tell me the stories of the people in the group. This man, he said, has a fire in his backyard every Sunday, just show up, no invitation needed. This guy over here, everyone drops off their key at his place when they're going on a holiday. Over here, this dude makes the best margarita... and on it went. I remarked, this is really cool, why do you guys do it? I was fishing for a reason why regular people from the neighborhood would care to gather and support one another (as if the church is the sole owner of community). My friend simply replied, to them, it was important to live and build a great neighborhood, and that started with relationships. You may not be surprised, but there wasn't a single Christian in the lot. Take a walk next time you can to that hole in the wall pub and learn a name or two. In the least, you'll share a good story about your neighborhood. But perhaps you'll receive an invitation to join community.

Not all allies are hidden in the pubs. Municipalities (especially in metropolitan areas) run programs, particularly for at risk demographics and neighborhoods. Conducting an environmental analysis of your neighborhood will reveal not only needs, but contributing agencies as well. When I was looking to become more involved in my neighborhood, I noted the obvious needs I could see, then I tried to discover what programs were *already* in place. It wasn't long before I connected with a city social worker devoted to the area. When we met up I said I was looking to build relationships and neighborhood programming. I was part of a church but wasn't looking to promote the church, just looking to go deeper into the needs of the neighborhood where I lived. Needless to say, when social workers develop trust and see someone willing to become participants to make the city better, they're very willing to both have a conversation and plug you into all sorts of activities. The focus to build relationship first, and to come to the table to join and build what was already in progress, developed a friendship that saw our groups participating in community BBQs, ESL programs, youth employment workshops, Christmas care packages, you name it.

Movements Need Collaborations

Consider these truths from my experience turning dreams real: 1) by yourself you're incomplete, 2) God will bring advocates and collaborators into your midst to help with the dream. Up to this point I've used individualistic language to build *your* dream. Individually, we have dreams and visions for better in our world—that preview of heaven *now*. Our dreams find critical value, potential, and power when they're connected into a church community. However, connections don't end there. Layers of collaboration exist beyond church community. If you don't know where they are commit the search to prayer. You'll be surprised whom God will place in your journey. Once an idea goes public, it's an invitation for the world to come and participate. How you work with others can make or break your journey. When the church is no longer the center, *cooperation* becomes the new means of participation.

To illustrate my ideas on collaboration, I will use social justice initiatives as examples. For complex problems, the church has taken a back seat. Government, NGOs, and secular organizations are at the forefront for many problems we wish to fix such as homelessness or human trafficking. Often these organizations have no interest in partnering with churches. It's not because they are anti-faith, rather, they're used to encountering faith groups who have ulterior motivations (such as proselytizing). In our post-Christian world the church no longer has inherited privilege, yet it often acts like it does. Churches try to own initiatives they know little about and twist their involvement to suit their own needs rather than meet the greater good of the problem. We need a different approach because in a post-Christian culture our actions help the world learn about the church they now know little about.

Look in the Mirror

When I wanted to address the needs in my neighborhood I opted to learn and support what was already at work. I came looking to partner and join, not to lead or insert my agenda. That helped me develop important relationships with key players in the community. Often the church doesn't approach collaboration with the same posture. We try to assume "ownership," relying on theological convictions that believe true justice only arrives when the church does. It's an understanding that presumes works are worthless if they are not accompanied with a salvation message (literally preaching). I've heard popular preachers proclaim that justice doesn't count unless a traditional evangelical salvation message is preached. "Why offer a glass of water to someone dying of thirst if they don't receive the eternal waters of salvation?" they bemoan. Wherever your theological convictions lie, "merely" loving people and offering a glass of water to the thirsty is a worthy and powerful witness to the gospel. It counts. And whether someone, a church, or an organization is aware of it or not, righting wrongs is kingdom work. Proclamation of Jesus is certainly a crucial component in revealing God's story, but it's mere clanging sound without embodied witness. So what approach should we take in collaborative efforts?

The first step is a work of repentance in our own hearts. In Isaiah 58, Israel is admonished for going through the religious motions while ignoring the importance of their activities to embody God's dream for his people and creation. Despite their religious convictions, God declares, *"you are living for yourselves...you humble yourself by going through motions of penance....no, the kind of fasting I want calls you to free those who are wrongly imprisoned and stop oppressing those who work for you. I want you to share food with the hungry and give clothes to those who need them. Then when you call, the Lord will answer, 'Yes, I am here.'"* It seems God cares about your activities in righting injustice, not your religious convictions upholding rules and regulations. God is interested in our spiritual acts of worship that aim to restore the ruins of the city, and not our vain religious offerings.

How to Collaborate - Join

My work in the area of human trafficking began after I saw a movie, or in this case a "rockumentary," called *Call+Response*. The injustice of human trafficking was wonderfully told through story and music. After the viewing I knew I had to respond. But rather than opting to support international efforts, and rather than thinking about launching my own NGO (which is the last thing you should think of doing), I sought after any local organization already doing good work. I found one, slowly developed a relationship with the organization, started to volunteer, and ultimately found a role to help with my specific skill set in board governance. I never would have found my role had I not connected in my first meeting and asked, "How can I help?" and not, "Here's what I want to do."

You have had moments where injustices were brought to your attention either through social media, the news, or even film. The first feeling is often a snap response, "I have to fix this wrong." That's normal, but it's also fleeting. Feelings do not lead to informed or lasting response. Sifting through sensational reporting and arming yourself with education about a particular issue are necessary first steps. When we arrive on scene to help, approaching with a humble posture to learn and support initiatives already working goes a long way to becoming entrenched with key players righting systemic injustice. It's one of the best ways to fix complex problems. You may be surprised by how many NGOs or government programs are addressing the issue you've just become aware of. Find them, and join them.

To help your idea move forward in response to injustice, and to help you collaborate with others, here is a summary of this chapter to consider.

1. Consider your own repentance first (Isaiah 58).
2. Start local. This isn't to discredit international work, but chances are you can find a considerable amount of activity already happening in your city on your issue.
3. Take inventory of your assets and capacity (individually and corporately).
4. Rethink justice. Justice doesn't show up when you do. You are invited to participate with the kingdom that's already at work.
5. Search for like-minded organizations already responding. Learn from them, volunteer with them, support them, bankroll them, collaborate with them.
6. Incarnate vs. One-Off. Churches have a habit of responding to justice or missions in seasons. With longer timeframes we can work to replace the sporadic "justice week" or "missions month" and form our congregations around ongoing

mission. Incarnate presence enables the possibility of longer timeframes that can support the years needed to right systemic issues.

7. Pray as you go.

Chapter 19

Pioneers & Church Plants

"The Christian mission is thus to act out in the whole life of the whole world the confession that Jesus is Lord of all." - Lesslie Newbigin

You may have your own dream, but it doesn't come to fruition by your lonesome (Prov. 15:22). The success of your idea hinges on locating disciples, partners, and collaborators. If you have none of these, don't move until your prayers have been answered for at least the disciples component. For me, collaboration and partnership were two reasons why my ministries didn't fail early on. They were critical for my survival and I would argue necessary to function in post-Christendom. My journey towards my first church plant started with a large denomination immediately after seminary. Being a little rough around the edges, and finding the conventional church service difficult to sit through, the idea of launching a new innovative church plant sounded like a good fit. After passing rounds and rounds of assessments upon assessments, the denomination and I parted ways (my ideas didn't fit their culture). What most prospective church planters don't know is that the crazier your ideas for community (which is to say the format of the Sunday service), the *less* likely you are to plant with an established denomination. Conventional church planting generally comes in *one* format. Out of the box ideas need not apply. Facing this system, and not wanting to relinquish my ideas, I did the dumbest thing a church planter should do—I struck out on my own.

Calgary Missional Church

When I started my first church plant I had no sending church, no denominational help, and no friends who wanted to come along for the ride. I wouldn't recommend this approach to anyone. God knew the plan lacked wisdom too. That's why by the grace of God, two small communities found me very early in my journey. Through our relationship we discovered our common heart for the community. Our friendships forged a new church gathering that found unity despite differences. We lasted nearly seven years, and when it ended most of the people remained connected.

My story may not be unique, but it was in stark contrast to the other church planters and ministries in the area. There were nearly half a dozen initiatives that sprung up around the same time in the artsy inner-city neighborhood called Kensington. What I found peculiar was how *few* of them connected with like-minded churches in their vicinity. Most stuck within denominational boundaries. Few sought the insight of community leaders. They were more concerned about their affiliations and methodologies than they were with building genuine relationships in the community. Collaboration wasn't a primary concern, doing the administrative work to launch a good service was. Of all the church plants in Kensington, *not one* remains (including mine although we lasted the longest at seven years). All but one closed after two years, and that one moved to another part of town. Their lack of desire to connect by relationships with practitioners in the vicinity contributed to their expected demise.

A different way to organize emerged around the same time these church plants were closing. A new ministry called The Mosaic sought to draw in practitioners and pioneers regardless of creed or affiliation. The intent was to build relationships first, rather than network. After, we looked for ways to support and work together specifically in a post-Christian culture. We wanted to know if it was possible to create a foundation that encouraged the sharing of efforts and resources, thereby giving small and sometimes unaffiliated kingdom expressions a better chance to survive. Usually, sharing money between churches is rare. This mindset starts to shift when relationships take precedence over affiliation, and we see the value of kingdom initiatives beyond denominational lines. It's our attempt to live in the "now but not yet" of post-Christendom. We haven't lost Christendom entirely, yet it's on its way out. The challenge is to take good ideas from Christendom and apply them in a post-Christian context.

Balancing between new and old paradigms slows our discovery for better ways to engage with the kingdom in a new culture. We incrementally try new things so we don't have to give up our familiarity with routines. It's like church planting ventures—they tend to come in one-size fits all packages. We train one pastor to run a Sunday service and shepherd a congregation. What we need instead are better ways to turn more dreams for better into reality. We need to let go and release the dormant priesthood. Here's what I mean.

Church Planting

It wasn't long ago when building a new church building was a viable strategy. There was a saying, "build it and they will come." A church could send out the lone church planter and within a year or two a congregation would emerge. In the 1950s there was enough

denominational cash flow to actually *build* a new building and fill
it with the people who lived in the community. Grandma attended
that church. The strategy worked because in Christendom everybody at least identified as Christian. It didn't mean they were prac-
ticing, but most everyone had a memory of going to church at some
point. The task was to remind these folks of the importance of their
faith and the church.

In the 1970s we started to notice that "build it and they will
come" wasn't working as well. Building a new church wasn't cost
feasible. Instead, we moved to one big church, and the mega church
era began to pick up steam in the late 80s and 90s. In the 2000s ambitious church plants could find moderate success, but with rented
space rather than purchased. Despite these shifts the core was the
same: train someone to deliver great services, plan for an awesome
service launch, bomb the target demographic with leaflets, and
on opening Sunday the seats would slowly fill. Essentially church
planting was an exercise in creating a carbon copy of the sending
church, only with a slightly different demographic. It's a spider organization creating one more spider.

Today "build it and they will come" still doesn't work. But instead
of embarking on the necessary changes to build new paradigms we
merely shifted from "build it" to "have it and they will come." Have
what? The all-important Sunday morning church service. In the
1950's this worked. Seventy years later only Christians readily respond to the Sunday morning offering. Addressing declining affiliation with robust church planting is a good idea. But if our attempts
only go so far as to change the package and location of a service, are
we improving the mechanism to our witness? Re-attracting lapsed
churchgoers or transferring switchers from other services means
we're just dipping into the shrinking pool. A strategy for Sunday

service alone doesn't work for the nones and dones because it relies on the erroneous assumption: majority culture wants what a church service offers.

To the churches that can afford it, church planting is an option to do something to address decline, but it falls short of broaching the core issues. We aren't solving fundamental problems of rugged individualism, multiplying discipleship, or replicating movements that embrace God's mission in the city and beyond. Before any endeavor of church planting we must always ask the question, "How does this fundamentally answer the question of joining God's mission?" Successful church plants therefore are not the ones that can grow a Sunday service by attracting lapsed Christians, but the ones that are deeply committed to their missional activities, including living and announcing the gospel in the places and spaces the church—the people—already exist. Instead of a question of mission, often church planting organizations try to figure out ways to mitigate the risk of the existing models. Less risk for new ventures means we can continue using old paradigms with success. One such mechanism is church transplanting.

Church Transplanting

I contend the vast majority of large churches do not actually participate in church planting, rather, they engage in *church transplanting*. A transplant could take the shape of a multi-site where nothing changes other than moving a few people to a different location. The preacher is still beamed into the place, and maybe the music too. More often, as multi-site becomes less popular, congregations cleave off a portion of their people to try meeting autonomously in a new location. Churches large enough to transplant understand it's a sustainable way to start something new. Sending hundreds of people to a new location means you also send the money and people resources for that new expression to survive. It's a viable strategy in risk management. But is a transplant the same as a brand new church plant? New plants come from new seeds, and develop their own DNA, expectations, and leadership structures. Transplants are cleaved off from the whole, retain the same DNA, but can grow into a new independent organism that could build others. I believe church transplanting is a viable way for large churches to operate as spiders sending out another spider. However, I challenge it's still not addressing the core need to create self-replicating movements that survive and thrive in a post-Christian culture. The answer to decline won't be found in replicating the same church from Christendom in a different location. We need different expressions that go beyond the contemporary Sunday morning Christian experience.

Common Transplants

A large church launched an evening service for their young adult demographic. Over the years the young leader grew the service to about 125. Those young adults turned into young parents and the Sunday evening service wasn't the answer anymore. It was time to shift, not for the sake of mission, but internal demand. A committee was formed and a search began for a new space that reflected the contemporary congregation. It so happened a closing church in the inner-city heard about the "church plant," and after some brief governance, bequeathed the entire building. Although this church self-identifies as a new church plant, there's little new about it apart from extricating themselves from the dominion of the old denomination (maybe that's all you need to do?). They shifted the same people from one location to another. The possibilities for reinventing their practices around place and presence were there, but ultimately the ingrained culture of consumer Christianity proved to be a powerful force to overcome..

Once they started in their new location things took off. They were the new cool church in town filling a demand for those Christians starved for a contemporary inner-city service. Overnight the service grew from one to two, and then three. There was no end in sight to their growth and in the words of their pastor they "could have gone to 800 people." That's when he threw on the brakes.

One Sunday the pastor declared from the pulpit that the church wasn't ready for 800. Rather than moving to four services he announced a different direction: he asked the attendees to *return to the churches they were coming from*. *All* of the growth was attributed to excited Christians transferring from other churches. In order to preserve the identity of their initial congregation, this pastor had to ask consumer Christians to stop coming. His rationale seems to have paid off as the church planted five years later. But have they answered the fundamental problem? Was their growth a result of a new expression connecting the gospel with non-Christians, or a spider church transplanting a spider? To be expected, it was the latter.

Will church transplanting solve our missional woes? There's certainly potential if those churches discover their calling and go to make disciples of all nations, alerting others to the reign of God in their midst. But often when we transplant we are merely creating a new way for Christians to find a different space to comfortably and quietly remain in the familiar world.

House Churches and Organic Communities
A different way to address the shackles of institutional tradition

is to deconstruct the entire system into its simplest form. House churches, neighborhood parishes, and the multitude of messy organic communities fall into this category. In theory, small communities are more conducive to address the failings of big, such as building strong relationships and centering purpose around neighborhoods. A lot of the ideas are great, in theory. But many know that small doesn't equal deep relationships. Nor does a neighborhood location mean good presence. There's a joke that the only thing house churches can do is "church done poorly." It's probably not fair, but it does raise the question of how we can shape the smaller into their own versions of thriving churches.

House churches often decry the legacy of the institution but wind up in the opposing ditch in the process. Common pitfalls include lack of clear vision, limited growth, ignoring liturgy and traditions, accountability, right teaching, and large impact. This is of course a generalization, but it does highlight the dangers. Often small is an excuse to stay that way while rejecting gathering. Yet we are called beyond our neighborhoods or networks by a commissioning that extends into the four corners of the earth. We also receive power when connected into the whole. Although small counts as church, if you have the ability to gather broadly with the multitude of saints, which in North America you can, don't deny this crucial forming opportunity. It may not be a weekly event, but it's necessary to remind yourself you're not alone, particularly in an age of marginalization. That could mean searching for a new community of saints you like to be around. The rationale of small and not "going to church," replacing it with, say, a community meal, may be great community building, but it's an anemic representation of the fullness of the body in your city. Jealously pursue the power and magnitude of God's combined church on mission by collaborating with like minds on mission.

Pioneering

Then we have the pioneers, the missionaries who embed themselves, and translate the gospel to a group, demographic, place, or
sub-culture. They don't fit any form or model because they create their own. If your dream or idea is connected to a sub-culture
largely disconnected from contemporary church culture, then you
are or will be a pioneer. While most church plants and transplants
still rely on the outsider to do the culture translation to fit in community, pioneers seek to live the character of Jesus in the places
conventional churches don't exist. Most of these expressions tend
to stay small, many struggle to survive, but if they stick around long
enough, they can experience similar levels of growth and transformations as the cruise ships.

Of course, pioneers have problems too, namely obscurity. It's
always a hustle as a pioneer. That usually means being alone on
the fringes where you lack proponents, people, and resources. You
run the risk of fading away into the fog if you operate too far away
from established community. The distinct lack of safety increases
the need to find other pioneers who understand what you're doing
by offering needed confirmation and extended community.

All of these expressions demonstrate how big God's kingdom
is and how much more we need to explore to join what is already
unfolding. If your community is small, ideas will gain longevity and
power in collaboration with like minds. When it's big, find those in
your midst already living mission without permission (the bright
spots). Come alongside, learn together, and build what's already
working. It's the easy win that pays dividends right away. By building trendsetters you can preview to those who prefer safety that the

kingdom has much more to offer. Only the chasm that discipleship bridges stands in the way of tipping an idea into a movement where the majority of people will call a dream their own.

One the keys I've discovered ministering in a post-Christian context is the untapped value of stories. Everyone has a story to share, we just need help finding our voice. That voice is drawn out through discipleship as we discover giftings and how they contribute to God's mission. When that happens, it acts as a catalyst to draw others into a faith journey. When someone new to community discovers a piece of themselves wrapped in a story a connection is made. "That happened to me," they say, as they open to conversations about how someone they know and trust confronted triumph or despair while chasing the fullness of their calling in Christ. This is a crucial foundational feature for community in post-Christendom. It's different than rooting a church in the story of the one preacher or experiences through programs or Sunday services. Not that they never work, but those consumable features lack the desired depth and appeal life-on-life relationships offer. Our culture is looking for deeper. We just need to patiently let God's mission flow through our lives and into the lives of others over the span of years, decades, or however long it takes. Do our churches have timeframes to accommodate this? Or are our measurements too focused on short-term gains?

Chapter 20

Measurements

"Measurements are hostile to Christian formation." - Darrel Guder

Chances are the idea you have for better includes daydreams of grand results. Lead pastors or church planters often have grand visions of filling stadiums or at the very least growing congregations, because *size* is the primary measuring stick in the contemporary church. Borrowed from the culture of consumerism, bigger equals better. When a business cracks $1 million in profit for the first time it's a celebration. God's kingdom, on the other hand, is not in the industry of sales or numbers. But that doesn't stop most from using similar kinds of metrics in our churches. Church planting language is full of metrics pertaining to multiplication thanks to books and conferences that reflect grandiose objectives. We don't value words like "additional" or "incremental," we hope for, and name our conferences "exponential".

Measurements are used because they give us some degree of control to quantify success and failure. However, it's hard to use numbers in areas where we have little precedent. The Western church lacks experience living in post-Christendom, so how can we even decide which metrics work with any degree of certainty? Is it harmful to use metrics? Or is it beneficial to know where we're going and if we've arrived?

Parable of the Harvest (Matthew 13:24-43)

When Jesus sends out the seventy he reminds them of the great work God has done before them. A great harvest is waiting but there's a shortage of workers in the field. The harvest and planting are up to God. We respond in faithfulness by entering the field to work (bear witness to the character of Jesus). The results, after showing up, are up to God too. As I said earlier, doing the work to turn dreams real matters most. Jesus (or Paul for that matter) would have provided clear instructions if numerical measurements were part of journey. But there are none—at least not numerical ones. That hasn't stopped established churches from operating with some manner of metric usually in the form of the ABCs: attendance, building, cash. If these were kingdom metrics pastors would be pressured to form the community around the function of these three elements. Which is what we see in practice, sadly. It's the Goldilocks conundrum of balancing consumer Christianity with kingdom priorities of living out our love for God, love for one another, and love for our neighbors.

Having said all of this, the obvious answer to address church decline is by *growing*. If we look back to the function of the church prescribed in Ephesians 4 we do have some mention of *building* of the body. Growth is evidence of health it would seem. The healthy body is one where Christians are faithfully living out their calling rather than being satisfied or placated in the pews. So how are we to approach planning or accommodating for growth? Good businesses will have very clear goals and objectives that inform strategies and tactics. A re-orientation of church measurement isn't an excuse to operate without a plan. But *what* we measure is important. The

ABCs tend to measure static snapshots of the community only on a Sunday morning. It lacks the ability to glean good data on how well discipleship is doing, how well the community is making inroads in the community, and how many nones are encountering the gospel story. Is there a different a way to determine if our dreams for better are on the right path? There are a few, and I think they have to do with digging deeper towards our foundation to create markers or milestones that work in post-Christendom.

Baptizers

If we must, I suggest we count baptisms. Baptism is a crucial formative mark in the Christian journey. I've looked at annual reports from the biggest churches in my city—I've been to a few of their baptism services too—and I've discovered a few things. Big churches are baptizing the most people. They tend to baptize more per capita as well. However, the total number baptized is still exceedingly small. For example, a church with an average attendance of about 5,000 reported under 80 baptisms over the year. That's under 2%, which is small but exceeds many other churches that baptize zero. The results get even worse when we look at how much money the church as a whole spends per baptism. I admit this is a broad figure, but if we take the total income of all churches and divide it by the number of reported baptisms, the results are a per baptism cost in America of $1.55 million,[50] and in Canada a figure of nearly $1.2 million.[51] If you think that's bad, I want to take it a step further. I'm not interested in the total number or the astronomical current cost. I'm interested in *who* we are baptizing. For that we need to pay attention

[50] Barrett, *World Christian Encyclopedia*, 774.
[51] Ibid, 170.

to the stories.

If you've ever gone to a baptism service in an evangelical church then you know how it works. Someone will share their testimony and then they are immersed. This comes after a meeting or some baptism classes. Sometimes someone even decides on the spot they want to be baptized and under they go. Next time you're at a baptism service listen close to the testimonies. You'll notice a common theme. Most say something like this, "...I've always been a Christian...and now I'm walking in obedience to Christ by getting baptized." We've established that churches baptize very few people per year, and those we do are mostly *existing Christians*. Often it's our own children. Make no mistake, all baptisms count, but those testimonies reveal *who* we are baptizing. What we rarely seem to hear are stories that go something like this, "I was never a churchgoer, knew little about faith, was lost, but miraculously Jesus found me and today I'm about to be baptized, so help me God!" Notice the difference? The last time I went to a baptism service in a large church of thousands (I'm not claiming this is empirical, but I'm sure it's close), they had *one* baptism, out of 25 that *year*, who wasn't an already churched person. This is a problem not because of the metric (1/25), but because it reveals how far the mission of that church travels.

If we only baptize a tiny fraction of our congregation, and only a fraction of that fraction include the dones or nones, what does that say about our witness? For one, it reveals where our Great Commission extends—no further than the reaches of Christendom. When we count baptisms we are forced to face what the average contemporary church faces—there is little mission beyond the pew. When we replace metrics reserved for Sunday morning with the number of people baptized who've never known Jesus, we get an instant feedback on how well we're doing joining the kingdom harvest in our midst.

Do a quick baptism count of your own community. What are the results? For many the answer will be close to zero. How can you fix this problem? Doing away with the ABCs overnight probably won't work. The answers will rely on righting systemic problems on what we believe is important in our churches. For that to transpire we will need patience that extends into decades and perhaps generations. In the meantime, there are easy wins that coincide with the bright spots strategy I mentioned earlier. Analyze the common denominators in the few people who are baptized with that story, "I was lost but now am found." Their transformation is often a result of deep relationship with someone, or a few, in the church. People already living out a calling to faithfully demonstrate the character of Jesus in their space and place, producing fruit with the people whom churches struggle to connect with. Build, resource, and learn from these pioneers. They are living out their ideas and dreams, and the result is kingdom wins for eternity.

The Three Percent

For me, witnessing baptisms is a huge indicator that goes a long way to legitimize even the most obscure kingdom initiatives. If I count anything, baptisms are a key metric in a post-Christian world. But should there be a number we strive for? When we read about building the body in Ephesians 4, is there a particular growth rate we should be aware of? An answer, surprisingly, exists in the early church. If I said *you can reach the growth numbers of the early church* in your community would you believe it? What if I said the possibility you can exceed the growth numbers of the early church is possible because you're already close? To achieve this momentum all we need is a little time.

Counting baptisms is one viable metric in a post-Christian context. But is there a number we should consider? When we read about building the body in Ephesians 4, is there a particular size it we strive for? The answer, surprisingly, exists in the early church. As we chase momentum and the building of the body, we could learn from the activity of that early church and their success. There's no Three hundred years is a long time. By comparison it's the difference between today and when Johann Sebastian Bach started composing. That's about fifty years *before* American independence. It's also approximately the number of years from the Day of Pentecost to the rule of Constantine. During that time the church grew from approximately 3,000 on the Day of Pentecost, to around 30 million a few decades after Constantine legalized Christianity.[52] When we calculate the year over year gain the early church experienced to reach those numbers over that time period, it equates to just over 3%. That means the *average annual growth for the early church was 3% per year.*[53]

Three percent seems small but it accumulates into multiplying growth figures over the course of generations, and in this case centuries. This is why we should be wary of using growth metrics and "exponential" language when they are coupled with short-term expectations. It's harmful because it misses real, yet small, momentum in the present that may be unobservable without decades of activity.

Stop for a moment. Count the people in your community then multiply by 3%. A church of 40 grows by maybe one person a year.

---

[52]   I'm using rough estimates for starting and ending numbers, but the point is the average yearly increase that is about the same.

[53]   Consult Stark, *"Rise of Christianity"*, 2011, for additional data.

Mega churches of 1,000 grow by 30 people. Not church transfer growth, but 30 new people baptized with testimonies of, "I never knew Christ, I never went to church, I was lost, but through relationships in this community, I am found!" What's your number? Does your dream for better put that within reach? Do you have a long run view of church growth and success? What we lack in patience luckily doesn't change the math. 3% sounds achievable because it is. Remember the mega church that could barely baptize 2% of their weekly attendance a year? Well maybe the news isn't so bad. Two to four percent is early church growth numbers. It's in fact movement state! Some churches can achieve this number through births alone (although I wouldn't rely on that strategy). Although the metric isn't cast in stone, it does offer a barometer test for your community. Movements of 3% may be panning out all around us as we reclaim practices like re-valuing presence and place in the neighborhood, along with timeframes for new expressions that span into generations. That's what's in reach when you live out your picture for better: you faithfully join the harvest field while letting God do the rest.

Part IV.

Tests & Enemies

"Where we learn to avoid the
threats that derail new ideas."

Chapter 21

Battle Lines

"Answers are closed rooms;
and questions are open doors that invite us in."

- Nancy Willard

They had barely left the Shire when the hobbits started to encounter enemies of all shapes and growing sizes blocking their path. From daring mountain peaks, cave orcs, monsters blocking the way, evil wizards, battles at Minas Tirith, Rohan, and the final epic encounter at Mordor, enemies stood in the path before they could reach their final destination. Each setup was a larger encounter than the previous one, making the reader question whether final victory was impossible.

When Luke Skywalker first encountered Darth Vader, he watched from afar as Vader defeated Luke's mentor, Obi-won, in a duel. It took three movies to build towards the final duel between good and evil. At the climax, Luke was defeated at the hands of the Emperor, until Vader unexpectedly switched allegiance. The audience breathed a sigh of relief. Balance in the force had been restored.

No adventure is worth its journey if it doesn't face adversity. We're interested in stories that mimic the human condition. We want to see how characters face insurmountable obstacles, but how they confront their own internal struggle as a person as well. The same process exists when ushering in new ideas for better. Every venture is fraught with challenges, tests, and enemies trying to hold us back from making the changes necessary to survive. Being alert for the common adversaries, including known impediments that we are sure to encounter, will help increase the chances your dream will turn real and thrive in a post-Christian world.

***

The Christian story is a declaration that evil has already been defeated. The forces both seen and unseen,[54] of powers and principalities,[55] have been defeated at the cross.[56] The epic struggle between good and evil was won as God condemned sin through the flesh of Jesus (Romans 8:3). The power of evil was robbed through the unique victory of death and resurrection at the cross. A new way of life, a story for the entirety of the cosmos, came to light with the new reality in the forgiveness of sins.

"The 'forgiveness of sins' was neither simply a personal experience nor a moral command...it was the name for a new state of being, a new world, the world of resurrection, resurrection itself between the archetypical forgiveness-of-sin moment...a face rooted...in Jesus' death, then revealed in his resurrection, and then put to work through the Spirit...." [57]

---

[54] Colossians 1:16
[55] Ephesians 6:12
[56] Colossians 2:13-15
[57] NT Wright, *The Day the Revolution Began*, 156-157

Although the ultimate battle has already been won, our own idolatry inhibits living out the fullness of our own calling. We can't control what culture does. What we can do, however, is change our own heart and witness. We must do the deep work to discover what areas in our own heart needs repentance. If we don't, we may wind up like the church in Laodicea.

Standing outside of a home he could hear people on the inside talking. He tried the door but it was locked. He knocked loudly and waited for someone to let him in. The noises from inside fell silent. Nobody seemed to be coming to unlatch the door. Surely, they must have heard him? He tried again and called out, "I'm at the door knocking, can't you hear me? Someone let me in!"

Evangelicals have long used this passage from Revelation 3 as an evangelism proof text. Jesus is knocking on the door of your heart, won't you open up and let him in? But Jesus isn't knocking on the door of the unbeliever's heart, he's knocking to enter a church gathering at a house in Laodicea. Jesus is trying to get in and the Christians won't let him! This section is a tough one that's meant not to deconstruct paradigms but to challenge them. Think of the ideas as alerts to the idols and beliefs in our faith that have become sacred at the expense of the Christian witness.

Ideology or Jesus

One factor that contributed to the decline in mainline denominations over the past four decades was the cultural shift towards secular liberalism. Evangelicals during this time held clear and identifiable principles that may have contributed to their comparative resilience.[58] At the time of this writing a stunning reversal is at

---

[58] See Wilkinson and Reimer, 2015. Bibby has written on this subject as well.

play. Not the resurgence of mainline traditions, but evangelicals succumbing to secularism, just on the opposite end of the political spectrum. Conservative evangelicals have married with secular conservatism at the expense of their gospel witness to outsiders. The evidence culminated in November 2016, and has been unraveling since.

The contested American presidential election saw the underdog Republican candidate Donald Trump become the 45th president. His win revealed both controversy and affiliation. The shocking factor was not Republican support, but how white evangelical Republicans *increased* their support for Trump's presidency. To outsiders, the character of the conservative evangelical witness was making bold statements. For example, Liberty University students erupted in cheers when Donald Trump was introduced by celebrity evangelical leader Jerry Falwell Jr., as the president "who bombs Muslims." You had the sense a deeply engrained cultural heritage was surfacing. Not a culture chasing the character of Jesus, rather one celebrating nationalism and secular conservative ideology. How does this happen? It seems the need to protect personal ideology and belief structures are immovable forces.

Conservative evangelicals were and are willing to overlook moral failures (one of many other issues) to laud a president for the *potential* of what could be done for their ideology. It seems more important to attain power and preserve ideology than it is to embody the subversive gospel message. This book won't dive into the profound problem of connecting patriotism with the gospel (it is one factor that's led to the systematic collapse of evangelicalism); however, any church that requires legislative *power* to legitimize their gospel witness is taking a markedly different approach than Jesus.

It's not just conservative evangelicals trying to elevate their public witness with unwavering support for a political agenda over Jesus. For the right: gays, guns, abortion, and nation (immigration). But the left too: secularism, the environment, globalization, etc. Religion and politics can be a messy mix. When we replace the gospel with our own gospel we live out Matthew 6:24. We cannot serve two masters, therefore let the witness you bear, and the beliefs you hold dear, embody the character of Jesus. What you represent as gospel is not about all that you oppose, but the character of Jesus that is worth living. How others perceive this character matters too. Returning back to the fundamental question, we ask, can we respond to our calling to help reverse church decline by translating the gospel in a language outsiders can connect with? What they think matters. A battle of good versus evil is in our midst, and sadly the church at times is on the wrong side.

Cynical

New ideas generate energy that some believe can feasibly change *the world*. It's electrifying to encounter someone with vision this bright. But often, our need to change is bred out of unhealthy hurt from past church experiences, and not out of a healthy intent to join the kingdom already unfolding. Many do not work through their questions and tensions, and instead leave the church altogether. When I co-launched my second church plant, the expression was something my city had never seen before. I mentioned this to an older pastor I rarely speak to, and rather than offering support, he admonished me, saying, "Everyone thinks they're doing something cool and unique when it's new." Although I was right—what we had was unique—the comment contained veiled wisdom. Anybody who's affected by the decline in contemporary churches can easily develop an unhealthy dose of cynicism. After finishing seminary,

I was that person, a loose cannon calling out the self-preserving antics of contemporary evangelicalism.

Coming off a fresh paradigm shift, and still reconstructing what it was I believed, I invited myself to a denominational training weekend featuring Alan Hirsch. His commentary was at times scathing, which to me was refreshing. To hear someone "tell it how it is," confirmed to me there were allies in the camp of discontent. Or so I thought. During the small group conversations, I laid it all on the line and lamented the direction of the denomination (and evangelicalism as whole) to Hirsch. He won't remember this, but his response to me was a formative moment in my ministry. "Brother, cynicism poisons the soul." Those words hit hard. I had work to do.

There's a difference between cynicism and the prophetic voice of discontent. The latter attempts to communicate the story of God into the contemporary in order to compel the community back into faithfulness. The former assumes the worst in all people and wields unhealthy suspicion toward the institution. I was ignoring the value of the vintage wine in the old wineskin. I had nearly become the new grad who thought his ideas were the best ideas, the latest feature to the kingdom that was sure to catch fire. It's easy for a venture to launch with antagonistic views of the established church. A lot of new ideas come out of discontent, and they can produce two diametrical responses: angry and triumphant, or meek and humble. Many wrongly launch out of a place of wounding from church experience. But those wounds coupled with the cynicism? That's crippling.

Remember when I said the dumbest thing a prospective church planter could do would be planting a church on his own? I was wrong. The dumbest thing is starting something new out of hurt.

If that's you, may I encourage you to work through the questions, the hurt, the bewilderment, and pause before launching something new. This is one of the few cautions that I have toward an idea. Watch out for the enemies of cynicism, pride, and anger.

Money

How many people from your church would you still be friends with if there was no Sunday service? How much of your journey, your dream for better, would you live out for free?

A declining church forces us to reassess what's important. You can determine that by following where tithes are spent—the money trail. The money trail will reveal the most important components. Usually it's the building and the inputs for the delivery of the service. Staffing and building are necessary to support the Sunday service(s). That leads to the question, are we eager to participate in alerting others to the reign of God beyond the church walls? Or do we look after the needs of our own first, and then if there's room "do mission?" What if there's little to no room?

Smart business planning will ask, "Where do you produce value for the target market?" Feedback loops for products and services give you a picture of what customers are thinking. (National Church Development attempted a form of this in their heyday in the 1990s and 2000s.) Churches are similar; particularly when resources go into the services, you want to ensure the money is being spent well. Unfortunately, this speaks volumes about our focus: we are more interested in ensuring we deliver some type of service to our parishioners than we are with interacting beyond the church walls. We deny mission and favor consumer comforts. We've even trained people to demand, "being fed by Biblical preaching." There's usually secondary value such as programs the church may offer, but to the people who are paying their tithe, there's a necessity to offer what they demand. Don't believe me? I'm not suggesting this, but if churches did a 180° turn and completely stopped offering a Sunday service, they would wind up with a near empty church. What does this say about the value we produce? A great service? If it is then you're in the wrong business. Strong discipleship breeds a community that values relationships with one another over expression. But we don't see the majority of our resources being poured into relationships. It's still that Sunday service.

Devaluing of Place

Consumerism celebrates individualism and the notion that your needs are paramount. When you combine a bunch of individuals, even around some shared identity, there's a habit to look after community needs first and solely. Consumers do not default to deny themselves for the sake of the other, let alone their neighbors. Churches often adopt a form of this worldview. It's the needs of the church first, and if there's anything left over, a little bit for the outsiders. We seem to understand that Jesus called his followers to love one another, which we get. The other half is the love for the other—our neighbor—which we struggle with.

I don't watch much TV, but I have seen every episode of The Simpsons. (Maybe it's because my mom banned me from watching it in the early 1990s.) I enjoy when the show critiques the modern church in its backhanded way. In Season 26, Episode 16, The First Church of Springfield was damaged and the rebuild wasn't covered by insurance. A handful of parishioners took it upon themselves to raise the repair money. Their strategy involved learning to count cards so they could covertly win on the blackjack tables at the illegal casino. During training, the team hits a rough patch, where their mentor, convenience store owner Apu, reinforces what's at stake by having them picture what will happen if they have to sell the church: the church knocked down to make room for an "atheist strip club." The shock of this image motivated the cohort to complete their casino ruse, and the church was saved. Turns out part of this story happened in real life.

While I was going through my assessment as a church planter, the largest evangelical denomination in my city was trying to think of ways to engage in the inner-city. Their existence was dominated by their ability to appeal to upper middle-class families living in the suburbs. They serve this segment very well. At the time they happened to own a piece of land that would have been exceptional as a downtown ministry. It was a Christian bookstore that started to fall on hard times given the emergence of Amazon. However, there was little vision to turn the space into a ministry/community expression. Instead the denomination stuck to their expertise—land banking—and sold the property to fund a new headquarters on the edge of town. There was nothing abnormal about the multi-million dollar transaction, but what's ironic was what replaced the bookstore. I doubt the result was known beforehand behind the scenes, but once the building changed hands (maybe more than once), the Christian bookstore was replaced by the latest "upscale" strip club. A space that could have been redeemed was sold to the highest bidder and is home to one of the city's most oppressive legal establishments where women contort for cash. Had they known the outcome, would this denomination have done anything different? Consider the value of place beyond the short-term as a way to invest in the ideas yet to be seen that will impact the city for tomorrow.

Another story of place took place during my first visit to the gorgeous castle city of Edinburgh. I'm a city person and I marvel at the function and history of urban centers. I was there in August when the Fringe Festival marches into town for a full month of whirlwind festivities, ranging from talents of fine artists to up-and-coming raw comedians from around the globe. It was one of many festivals as Edinburgh, so I've been told, now seems to call any gathering of people a "festival." Running marathons in the summer are "festivals." The "Book Festival" was across the street from the flat where I stayed. I ran into Richard Dawkins there, he's taller than you'd expect. Apart from the unseasonal cold, everything about the city was electrifying and a pleasure. The beautiful people, the attractive accents, the walkability of a city, the views, inventive food, and a place that served a worthy espresso. Like on my other visits around Europe, I made a point to check out the churches.

One day, I was walking down one of the main streets and my friends shared a story about a church lingering on their block. None of the locals knew much about the church, nor were any of the parishioners from the area (which happened to be in the heart of downtown). What the locals did know, however, was that the church was for sale. Not because they're going out of business, rather they were *expanding*. Edinburgh, like many European cities, has an intensive process prior to the sale of any property, particularly those of historic value. The community is notified and in many cases will have a say on whether or not a sale can proceed. This is a chance for the neighborhood to weigh in on whether the new owners would be a good fit. Most city blocks in Edinburgh, and Europe for that matter, are not linear like in North America. You don't have a row of houses, an alley, and then another row. City blocks are arranged in, well, blocks, with buildings backing into each other. In this setup, everyone shares an inner courtyard. That means sound from one building would travel with ease into the others, most of which are hundreds of years old and generally lack the same soundproofing we'd see in modern construction.

As word travelled about the sale, concern mounted. Not because of the sale itself, but because of the buyer: a night club/pub. Four stories of late night hootenanny echoing throughout the front and rear of the building. The church didn't bat an eye. To them they were simply trying to liquidate an asset to serve their own need to find a larger space on the outskirts of town. The neighborhood, however, banded together, united in their concern about the proposed sale and how it would affect neighborhood dynamics. The decision for the sale happened one evening before a real-estate arbitrator. The community, including the local police and politicians, versus the church and the businessmen representing the club. What an incredulous and sad juxtaposition between neighborhood and church.

When they told me the story I had trouble fathoming how it was possible a church in a neighborhood as incredible and full of rich history as downtown Edinburgh could be so utterly disconnected from the people around them. But deep down I understood why, as this church looked like most churches from my context. Here too many churches are disconnected from their place, and struggle to provide for or even see the value of the local neighborhood. We have become fragmented from our connection to place, and therefore our posture defies our preaching to "love thy neighbor." We barely know who lives next door, let alone on the next city block.

In the end the church lost their appeal. Much to their chagrin, but much to the delight of the neighborhood. I inquired a couple years later to see what had happened to the church and the building. The story has a happy ending. The church did indeed sell, but it wasn't to a night club. Today a dance and art studio creates beauty in the city, something the church only did for themselves. The loss of institutional privilege, coupled with the rise of individualism, has led to the devaluing of proximity and the normalization of privatized faith. It turns the gospel from chief story in God's redemption plan, to one that only serves the needs of the declining church.

Chapter 22

Rules That Matter

"Then Jesus said to his disciples, 'Whoever wants to be my disciple must deny themselves and take up their cross daily and follow me.'"
- Luke 9:23 (NIV)

*H*is younger brother became obstinate. His work ethic declined on the family homestead. His gloomy disposition hung over the household, and it reached its height the day he demanded a portion of inheritance from his father. He wanted to leave his role and responsibility in the family to go make a name for himself in the world. Surprisingly, the father relented to his demands. The younger brother went away to his escapades.

Months passed without word about the younger brother. His last known whereabouts were unknown. As concern mounted, the family gathered to decide what to do. They agreed a search would begin, and the elder brother would accept the task. Off he went, tracking through questionable crowds, long desert roads, and dark corners of big cities, weeks then months passed without a clue. But then he caught his break. Someone matching his brother's description was working deep in a far off countryside. With determination, he checked every farm the further he travelled, just in case his brother would appear. As hope dwindled, one evening he turned towards a dilapidated swine farm as a figure in the distance toiling in the mud caught his eye. It bore instant recognition. He quickened his pace and when he came within earshot he was sure. "Brother! Brother! I've finally found you! I've been searching for months! Everyone has been worried sick. Will you come home? Dad's going to be thrilled when you show up! Let's go home, it's time to celebrate...."

It's a happy ending but that's not how the story of the Prodigal Son is written. The brother doesn't leave everything in search for his kin. He doesn't even celebrate his return. Instead he sulks in the corner and points to how he stayed true to his duty and expectations. He thought his quiet obedience to the traditions would protect his status. He was indignant when the Prodigal was celebrated upon return. "How could they?" he thought. "I followed all the rules!"

Absolutes

Do you have a list of non-negotiable beliefs? What's on the list? Sola scriptura, abortion, gay marriage, prayer in schools, evolution, drums in the worship service, preacher in blue jeans, not enough preaching, preaching isn't Biblical enough, the Trinity, the rapture, open theism, literal hell, women in ministry, women in yoga pants, men in yoga pants? Where do you draw the line? How do you draw a line?

In a post-Christian world truth becomes individualized and relative, yet I believe it's still necessary to cling to certain foundations. Jesus didn't come to abolish all traditions. However, he had no problem dismantling rules that favored position over people. Today, I would argue many contemporary traditions have a non-negotiables list that's too long. I'm all for having church belief systems.

My question is, why do we fight so hard over the list? Jesus said the gospel is so simple that even a child could understand it (Matthew 11:25). What are the simple yet important pieces? I believe there's one: *the incarnate Christ.* He is the Capstone to God's story of hope and redemption. When Jesus intercedes into the history of humanity everything changes. Incarnation is our identity and invitation that compels us, dare I say, forces us, to pursue constant innovation to join the kingdom already unfolding in our midst. Joining is different from the posture of Christendom where we sit and wait, resting in the laurels of inherited authority that rule making provided. We have the fullness of the kingdom glimpsed in Jesus, but live in tension knowing that evil still exists. God's kingdom has yet to come to full fruition, yet God is with us as we journey to discover the fullness of our humanity. Do our traditions and beliefs empower others to discover the fullness of their own humanity? Or are they used as cruel dividers to differentiate who's in and who's out of community?

Traditions vs. Relationships

Doctrines, beliefs, or traditions combine to uphold the ideals of an institution. Leading a culture shift, however, requires tough decisions that challenge these long-held systems. They include deciding which pieces of the institution to retain and which pieces to discard. Traditions have value, but that value is lost when they take precedence over people.

Jesus routinely rejected the arguments of the religious elite who were too eager to elevate their pristine records while failing to see the value in people. His actions and words would challenge even the most celebrated pastor of today. What would Jesus say about expectations and rules in your congregation? We know any kind of change is hard, and moving forward from long-held beliefs and traditions is harder. Rather than change, churches often posture inward in a protective measure against what it deems to be bad influence. In other words, they don't think it's important to actively reach beyond the assumed hallowed church walls. Some are so crass as to conclude it doesn't matter what outsiders think. It's better to expend energy protecting a lost way of life and privileges than protecting original ideas. Yet to be a witness of Jesus doesn't mean we are the possessor of all truth.[59] We should be asking questions like "How can we be faithful witnesses?" and "How can we live out the character of Jesus to our world?" and "What do we share in common with our neighbors?" This process doesn't mean giving up our identity, but it does mean we should be concerned with how outsiders receive our message. We need to know whether our traditions are inhibiting us from participating in God's mission.

Rules Hurt

I want to share a story from my friend Connie Jakab.[60] We are currently co-leading a church plant called Cypher Church (more on us later). I asked her to share a story about rules and people that she experienced years ago as a youth leader. You may resonate with her story.

> *"I was new to ministry and had a team of Bible college students interning with me at my church for the summer. One morning I had a conversation that I've never been able to forget. One of the students came into my office, shut the door behind him, and tentatively sat down. I could tell*

---

[59] Newbigin, *The Gospel in a Pluralist Society*, 12.
[60] Visit Connie's website: https://conniejakab.com/

he was about to tell me something serious. Then it unraveled. He began to unravel about his struggles being gay and how he felt it was time for him to come out of the closet. As a new pastor in my 20s, coming from an evangelical tradition that rejected homosexuality, I wasn't sure how to deal with this young man's struggle and his position as an intern. What I chose to do that day haunts me. I laid it out in black and white terms. His choice was either to abandon his decision to embrace his homosexuality and walk in God's favor as a straight man, or walk out my office door and never come back. He left, and he never came back.

To this day I wonder where he is and what could have been different if I had expressed the love of Christ to him rather than the religious rules, steeped in fear, that I was taught. He's not the only one who's faced a similar interaction in a church. Instead of just one, multiply him by the millions from the LGBTQ community who are constantly bombarded by conservative messages that seek to deny them basic human rights and protection."

Is the institutional church acting like modern day equivalents of the Pharisees and Sadducees? The critical issue Jesus had with the religious elite was the love they had for *rules over people*. It was more important to retain power than it was to value people. It was better to believe in the right things and go through the religious rites than it was to break convention and value the person as the image bearer they were. It was more important to preserve a way of thinking, along with power structures, than it was to obey the commandments to love. How many of us rigorously defend our way of life and religious ideologies? We must posture ourselves to be less like the Prodigal's older brother, who followed all of the rules, because in the end it was the wayward son who was celebrated.

Chapter 23

Tent Meeting

"What has cost God much cannot be cheap to us"
- Dietrich Bonhoeffer

*F*or years, a big tent would pop up in the middle of summer in a park near my home. The first time I saw it I stopped in my tracks in utter bewilderment. For a full week, an old-style revival tent would hold daily VBS and evening services, advertising across the neighborhood in mailer bombs. I never figured out who put it on, but I know it wasn't a local church. Someone from this ministry believes they're fulfilling their evangelism duty with an empty tent. In Canada, even in my conservative city, it's been well-over half a century since a tent meeting successfully attracted curious attendees, and a full century since it led to, well, a revival. The tent hasn't made a return for a few years, another victim of the lost church era.

There was a time when you could set up a tent with miraculous transformative results, but times change. In the 1960s and 1970s, evangelical churches found relative success in their weekly altar calls, parading new believers down for a "decision" of faith. Billy Graham had mass success speaking at packed stadiums and leading thousands to Christ. Today tent meetings barely exist, altar calls following a fiery sermon are rare, and stadium gatherings are full of the already churched. The post-Christian world doesn't think to attend a revival meeting at the local park. They are looking for answers, just not at a church service. That hasn't stopped contemporary churches from responding in new ways. The seeker sensitive movement sought to reclaim lost Baby Boomers and was successful in a manner. But it too stumbled. Discipleship has always been weak in seeker sensitive models of church. Relying on attraction continues today for churches who can afford to produce services and programs with "excellence." We haven't found a method that works in a post-Christian world, but at least every generation seems to be open to trying something new. That's why your idea for better is desperately needed. We need to test existing paradigms in Christendom to figure out what is inhibiting us from connecting with the world in new ways.

Adjusting Timeframes

Jesus spent more than two years with his group of followers discipling them for the work they were to do. We've already established that despite our want for discipleship it's hard to build disciples who in turn disciple. Why? Consider yourself for a moment. Let's assume you have been discipled well to begin with (many leaders have not), and have the drive to disciple others on top of whatever duties, job, or life you have. If Jesus took two years how long will it take you to venture with one? For example, let's say you disciple one person in two years. I'll also assume that the person you disciple will in turn disciple another. So after year two you have two people who have been discipled (you and the other person). If this process repeats, after *two more* years you potentially have four discipled people, and so on. Eventually, this cycle leads to exponential growth that seems appealing, but hang on. It's been four years, and only four disciples have emerged. How many of your ministries, visions, church programs, etc., have a longevity of four years? Let's assume those four years with disciples was a journey between good friends who were already familiar with Christianity. What happens when we venture with one of the religious nones? How long will that take? Assuming someone who's never connected with Jesus or the church before, you're not starting with discipleship. You're starting a simple relationship. (Careful how you use nomenclature. Don't call relationships with people who are supposed to be your friends "pre-disciples" behind closed doors. That turns genuine relationships into metrics.) Barring the miraculous conversion experience (which seems rare), how many years do you spend with the one none before that none is ready to disciple others? For a Christian it was two years. For a none is it three years? Five years? Never? Are we ready for new timeframes for genuine discipleship that extend into *decades?*

In post-Christendom, incarnating presence in your own neighborhood, where you must gain trust as a co-creator in the hopes and dream of the neighborhood (and therefore its people), takes years, perhaps decades (or so I've been told, I'm only in my first decade in my own neighborhood). We need patience for this renewed expectation. If we take the risk to embark on the journey to see our dream of better stretch beyond ministry to career Christians, our ideas need to withstand tests that extend generations.

What is the Church?

Our actions matter, but so do our words. In organizations, activities and functions need to match vision and dreams or confusion emerges, hampering success. Postures count, and some need to shift, especially if we want outsiders to grasp what we're doing.

Even though it may seem like a trivial adjustment, changing language that contradicts our actions is necessary to reverse the trend of our declining footprint.

How would you define the "church?" I have an early childhood memory of my dad teaching me a rhyme complete with actions. You may know it: "Here is the church, here is the steeple, open the church, here are the people!" I can't think of any churchgoer who would genuinely equate the church with the building or the Sunday service. But often that's not what we mean when we say it. Although most believe the church *is* the people, we also interchangeably reference the *church* as the building and the activities contained within. We've personified buildings to be "the church," saying things like, "Come to church, I'm going to church, and what church do you go to?" The correction is simple: replace the word "church" with the nouns we're referring to. "Come to service, I'm going to the church building, what church are you a part of, I have worship in the morning." This subtle shift makes an important impact that shapes culture. It supports the belief that the church is the people—the living body of Christ—working together beyond just a Sunday service to join God's dream unfolding in the neighborhood, city, and beyond.

Leaders in particular must pay attention to our actions and words. We can't preach one thing and do another. For example, we cannot call the church (the people) to mission if every Sunday service those people just sit and watch while the chosen few lead, play, and pray. The professional clergy run the show and the music leaders do the music. It seems you need qualifications to hold certain positions. Church leaders call people to become more engaged, but continue to demonstrate in our practice that only the few are qualified. We've trained average churchgoers to think, "I pay my tithe, let the leaders do the work on Sunday." That leaves leaders under constant pressure to continuously find volunteers for expected programming, and worse yet, exhausted from doing too much. Is there a better way?

This is a good time to broach a related question about church. Simply, "What is the church?" What items or elements need to be included in order for a community to be a legitimate church? Are the necessary parts worship, Jesus as head, Holy Spirit as regenerative, preaching as core, celebration of Eucharist, or confession? Or maybe it's less about the parts and more about the things you do? Helping the poor and the widows, selling our possessions, living in community, eating together, singing songs together. Perhaps it's how many people you have? Two or three gathered in Christ's name, 12, 24, 100? Is it institutional? Hierarchical? Historical? Is it Ethiopian Coptic, Byzantine, Roman Catholic, Anglican, charismatic, evangelical, Pentecostal? Would a weekly meeting together over barbecue count? Does a random gathering of friends over a meal constitute church? One small group? A once a month hip hop cypher? Perhaps all of the above? When our assumptions of what constitutes church take over, we start to draw the classic religious line between who's in and who's out. It also means someone new either has to learn the culture or follow the right rules to fit in. God's test to belonging is much wider.

Consumerism

Perhaps the biggest challenge to our identity is the subversive gospel and the mission of God versus individualism and consumer ideology. In the West, if changing culture relies on a change of the heart and head, what are the big pieces that need to be challenged? It's that first place we go with the lottery dream: an ideology called

"The American Dream." For many it's *the pursuit* in their lives. The heart of the "American Dream" is a notion your needs matter most. As consumers we can buy anything we desire and we deserve to fulfil those desires. Contrast that to the Christian tension of denying ourselves and picking up our cross to follow Jesus. The gospel life points in the opposite direction from the "American Dream" life. Does your community face this tension? Recall, resilient churches are the ones who can offer a church culture that largely resembles the mainstream. Churches condone (knowingly or unknowingly) consumerism so long as a few attributes are adhered to. It's as if we're largely unconcerned with how people live so long as they're showing the right actions on the outside. You can chase the "American Dream" so long as you show up to the Sunday service, give a little money, oppose certain moral failures, and use the right Christian language. It's as if what happens with your spiritual heart is of no concern.

Rather than catering to the individualized Christian experience (the Goldilocks conundrum), what does it look like to live like Jesus in the neighborhood? Nobody dreams about winning the lottery and driving their life straight into the pavement. It's the opposite: when given a chance we all dream about the best possible life, one without impossibilities. We certainly get caught up in dreaming of *my* best possibilities, with fancy cars, vacations, and a new house. Eventually we reach that point where we think of other people too. Your daydream for the best for you eventually includes the best *for others,* and demonstrates the reality that you are connected to a dream bigger than your biggest dream. Dreams fall short when we put ourselves at the center, because by ourselves we are incomplete. Rather, God's dream for all of creation invites you to belong in the unfolding hope that is to come—God's dream fully restored on earth as it is in heaven. But living out your dream, like any worthy journey, requires you to give up something in the process in order to emerge victorious.

If you knew a way to mobilize more people to get excited about God's mission in their place and space, to become disciples who disciple, would you see this kind of change through? Would you do it if it meant giving more power to the people and less for yourself as leader? Would you see this kind of change through even if it meant less music, shorter preaching, no preaching, or even fewer services? These kinds of changes would come at a cost: the quintessential consumer Christian will find an easier experience at the groomed service a short drive away. But would it be worth it if your community, your idea, led to a radical embodiment of God's mission in the neighborhood and beyond? Something to think about.

Chapter 24

Leadership

"Everyone gets to play." - John Wimber

*W*illow Creek Community Church grew to mega proportions riding on the success of the seeker sensitive model they catalyzed. Their success also had three noticeable impacts on contemporary churches big and small. The first saw the replacement of discipleship in favor of leadership development. It is, after all, the Leadership Summit, not the Discipleship Summit. The second, purely through market driven factors, the seeker sensitive model condoned racial segregation by maintaining congregational sameness while ignoring the problem of race inequality.[61] What is incredible about this distinction is how it was achieved. Mega churches gained success by implicitly retaining racial segregation through market driven approaches. They were (and still are) widely successful at creating programs and spiritual experiences carefully targeted to exclusive demographics.[62] Third was the goal to pursue rapid church growth.

---

[61] See Emerson, *Divided by Faith,* 2006. White Protestant churches are among the least diverse and have maintained racial segregation equivalent to the Jim Crow era.

[62] For example, Rick Warren's Saddleback Church relied on successfully attracting a demographic they targeted labeled, "Saddleback Sam." Although the homogeneity principal has been a strategy for sustainable mission work and church planting for decades, it produces congregations that look the same.

Not that every pastor embracing the seeker sensitive model wanted to be a mega church, but an inherent purpose was to *grow* congregations. In order to achieve this goal, correlating strategies need to be implemented. Churches began organizing themselves like corporations rather than, well, churches. To help with the growing need to run competent organizations, Willow Creek developed the Leadership Summit. I remember attending a simulcast and learning a lot of ways to improve my business. Translatable church development skills? Not so much. To their credit, although it took about a decade, the visionaries of the Leadership Summit realized the disconnect between producing leaders versus disciples. The two are decidedly not the same, despite references that treat them synonymously. Scripture lacks a leadership commission; Jesus didn't call the disciples to go and make leaders of all the nations. I wish I had realized this earlier on in my ministry.

I was sold on the leadership idea when I started in vocational ministry. For my first church plant I thought the answer to resiliency was finding and building more leaders. What I was really after was a critical mass of people to mitigate the risk of the new plant. I would lament, "If only a church would send, three, two, heck, even one leader, the ministry's potential would increase." My desire for more leaders was a reflection of the leadership development culture that still exists today. It assumes that healthy leaders will translate into success (or resiliency). However, growth is not the direct result of successful leadership development. Rather, it increases internal capacity to run programs. For many churches, the primary purpose in leadership development is not to release people out for the sake of God's mission, but to generate more and better managers to match internal needs. Leadership training imparts skills specific to church needs. It's a development in organizational competency, not the release of giftings in the body. What's preventing the contemporary church from initiating necessary change to build the body and increase discipleship to survive and thrive? We need to release the potential of those gifts instead. It's the answer to the problem we encountered at the beginning of this book: release the people. We have to unlearn and challenge leadership development so it becomes, or is replaced by, discipleship building. We've organized the contemporary church using corporate models of leader development. That's to be expected, but it must come a distant second to solid replicating discipleship activities. Given the contemporary church orientation towards leadership development paradigms, we need ways to change within the current construct. For that, let's ironically look to the corporate world for some insight.

Management

Businesses, like churches, fail when they are unable to face changing market trends. In *The Innovator's Dilemma,* Clayton Christensen analyzed companies that experienced catastrophic failure. One of the findings, and a leading cause of failure, was great *managers.* That's right. The most talented managers, brought in to address a current problem, wound up making the problems worse in the long run. Why? It turns out managers are built to maintain status quo, not propel organizations forward. Managers work in the present, understand how a company ought to function, and execute strategies to remain resilient when disruptions arrive. The top managers found a way to maintain and sometimes improve despite market shifts. Conversely, managers are unable to see looming threats, nor are they gifted to lead change. By the time a problem is finally understood it's too late, and the company fails.

A major contributing factor preventing churches and denominations from lasting change is church leaders. Not any one in particular, rather the *kind* of leader that seems universal in churches—the shepherding pastor. Churches tend to hire and develop the shepherding gift. Key attributes in today's pastor are the ability to care over the flock and lead a service (preach well). The result is a local church culture run in much the same way as businesses facing market shifts—by managers who are doing all they can to address decline, but are the wrong people to lead change. Change agents are not inherently shepherds. What we need stems back to good discipleship that seeks to build the unique gifts and callings within body while going deeper in the love for one another.

Priesthood

The Great Commission and Great Commandment combine to establish the platform of gospel witness. It's an invitation for all believers to embrace, not just qualified staff or leaders. Good Protestants supposedly believe in "the priesthood of all believers." However, in application there's a problem. We don't have a priesthood, rather we struggle with something called the Pareto problem, where 20% of the people do 80% of the work. Although we have commandments from Jesus to bear witness, and a function as church to build the body with everyone's gifts, in reality our ecclesial structures prevent this from happening. Centralized leadership is designed to *preserve* central authority. It's the institutional power and identity that pastors (managers) maintain from Christendom. Although technically centralized leadership structures are open to new leaders, the barriers to entry are high. There's a ceiling for how high the priesthood in the average church can go. We call it "lay leadership". To compound matters, lifelong Christians have been trained to rely on central authority and think less about how their gifts and calling can contribute to God's vision for the church. It's my grandma in her old neighborhood church never once considering what role she may have to engage in God's mission. Her duty ended with showing up on Sunday or making creampuffs for the bake sale.

Unleashing the dormant priesthood should be a primary objective of any church or community leader. It will challenge inherited (but eroding) leadership structures and power; however, those factors are eroding with Christendom anyway. Not mobilizing the dormant priesthood will further prevent the church from making the necessary changes to survive and thrive. One way to organize and potentially help build the kind of priesthood (discipleship) that is ready to live out gifts and calling involves flattening leadership structures. Along with distrust of religious institutions, a post-Christian culture will embrace leadership structures based on relationship rather than inherited positional authority. When you decentralize, the only power you have is what people give you. That's much the same in the world, where the church has little to no say in the everyday lives of people, but by relationship and presence in the neighborhood, we can gain equity and trust in the day-to-day.

Qualifications

Decentralizing also means a practice to decrease qualifications of who is a "leader." I contend the qualifications to live out your calling, or realize a dream within the context of your church, is simply your faithful response to go. Current leadership qualifications are much higher, at the expense of inhibiting the potential of the priesthood. Seek to release more people to be the hands and feet of the church even if that means the central structure has less control. This approach is widely successful in countries without the legacy of the institutional church. The church in China doesn't multiply exponentially because they require house church leaders to be denominationally trained and hold four-year degrees. But that's exactly what we do in North America. Church planters need significant qualifications to carry the moniker. As the church struggles to exist on the margins, the road to thrive includes strategies like church planting. However, for conventional church planting the entry requirements are astronomical. Don't believe me? Here's an excerpt from the desired qualifications that a large church posted in their search for a potential church planter.

• Experience in a multi-staff setting

• Participated in the leadership of a church building program

• Assessed and endorsed as a church planter through a recognized process

• Served as an apprentice in and/or experience as a church planter

• Experience in cross-cultural settings

• Ordained[63]

• Master of Divinity

• Five years' church experience

• Develop missional DNA

• Experience managing a leadership team

• Recruit community for a core to support launch.

• Procure facility and start up necessities for eventual service.

In case you're keeping tally, this list *exceeds* the qualifications of Jesus Christ! I know when hiring you put everything on the wish

---

[63] In this denomination that was a way to say males only.

list in hopes of getting close, but this is an example of the incredible barriers we place on potential leaders and church planters. The list didn't even include all of the other implicit assumptions for planters. For many denominations church planting is a strictly male enterprise, a relic of patriarchy that sticks around despite the function of the church being *gifts*-based not gender-based.[64] Denominations also include assessment after assessment to vet candidates. If you make it past this point you'll enter a cohort with other church planters, or simply start interning at a larger church for another year. During this time you'll put together those plans and strategies, and visions and dreams, to get ready for launch. Once all of this is complete there needs to be enough commitment from the sending church so a church service can begin. That's a two year commitment usually (sometimes more) for full salary and expenses to run the service. Ignoring the monetary cost of this endeavor,[65] it's no surprise only a handful of people make it. And for good reason. Most churches only know how to plant a church in a "build it they will come" model that's very expensive to replicate. A sending church or denomination will ensure their investment has the best chance of "bearing fruit" or becoming self sufficient.

In the example of church planting, what if one of the solutions would be to let anybody plant a church? I'm intentionally going to the opposite end of the spectrum, but that's just it, there's a spectrum we use to release and qualify church planters. In every church and denomination the primary leaders and elders are gatekeepers who decide who qualifies and who doesn't. When it comes to king-

---

[64] Women are included in every gift outlined in Ephesians 4.

[65] My own rough estimate for a church plant of 100+ congregants exceeds $250,000. That figure includes all assessments, salary during training, a guarantee for at least two years support, sunk capital costs to hold a great service, but not including the required four year bible degree.

dom momentum, we need to open the gates to recognize more people who are living out their picture for better. To do so we must let gifts speak louder than leadership training materials. The re-orientation of mission, and the test to our existing church structures, must embrace a return to a foundation of discipleship and not strategic models. Get the relationship part better, and we will have a mechanism to develop mission competency in our communities. Not everybody can be a lead pastor of a church of 25, 100, 250, 2,000 – but we're not looking for more people to fill declining roles. We need an orientation that accumulates smaller ideas along with a framework that enables more people to live them out with support. That process may come at the expense of losing some inherited privilege and status (for existing leaders), but that also means the legacy we leave won't be one where there are fewer churches than we inherited.

Part V.

Failure & Reward

"Where we prepare for the worst
and receive the best...maybe."

Chapter 25

Failure, Obscurity, Loneliness

"On the field of the Self stand a knight and a dragon.
You are the knight. Resistance is the dragon."
- Steven Pressfield

Taking the plunge to live out your dreams will mean encountering times of defeat and moments when you're scared stiff. You want to try something new but you aren't sure how it will be received. The elders won't go for it. The small group will reject it. None of your friends will support you. Or maybe the congregation is in a happy safe rhythm and disrupting the calm will cost you your job. After all, what will people think if your idea fails? "That will never work" or "I could never do that" are common internal battles that emerge when an idea reveals itself in infancy. Along with self-doubt are all the naysayers who emerge when your idea goes public. They bemoan the risk, potential loss, and the mere notion of challenging the status quo. Often, those you thought would be on your side, excited for something new, will be against you. Those whom you never considered as allies will emerge as co-conspirators. Innovation from established norm isn't an easy task to lead or live out. You'll want to quit multiple times along the way. You will start, re-start, and especially fail because failure is normal. I hope your dream and the love for each other triumph, but it's possible your idea won't work at all, or in the way you expect. There will be times when failure gains enough ground that you're left wondering whether you will survive. But don't be deterred. If you triumph, good. If you fail, that's OK too. Death is an inevitable and necessary part of every journey worth living. Death paves the way to resurrection. Death is the signal an old way is passing, and although you may emerge scathed, a triumphant new creation awaits. In death is a resurrection-sized hope. Ours is inextricably tied to the death and resurrection of the Savior. In the temporary defeat of the cross emerged the risen Christ, who defeated the clutches of death. He tore the veil in two so we may experience our own rebirth in our hearts. Cling to this truth as you enter the inevitable seasons of desert and failure. Every journey has them.

Failure

Entrepreneurs have one thing in common: they're all failures. As you turn more and more ideas real, eventually you'll face a failure or two (or seven). In fact, think of it as an expectation. Innovator, entrepreneur and business magnet Elon Musk is one of the world's leading inventors, challenging and changing more than one industry at a time. Known commercially for his role building online payment system Paypal, and the automotive company Tesla, Musk is very public with his experiences in failure. I remember one such moment in 2015.

Elon also heads SpaceX, a company that has an out of this world mission: *"...revolutionize space technology, with the ultimate goal of enabling people to live on other planets."* [66] In order to make this dream reality, SpaceX must innovate rocket propulsion systems, namely making rockets reusable so launches are cost effective. As the company started to expand their program, the size of potential failures was also amplified. For one, nobody had successfully reused a rocket sent into space before. SpaceX wanted to not only reuse their rockets, but they wanted to land them on a floating barge in the middle of the ocean! Their first attempt to accomplish this monumental feat was broadcasted live for the world to watch. Maybe you've seen the pictures. There in the dead of night in the middle of the sea a tiny floating barge bobbed up and down in the waves. Suddenly, the sky illuminates as a rocket comes into view, automatically fires its landing thrusters to slow the descent, and for a split second success looks imminent...until the rocket turns sideways and crashes into the barge. Fail.

Most businesses try to hide failure. Certainly, the last thing you want to do is *celebrate* failure. However, that wasn't SpaceX. The unsuccessful failed landing led to a SpaceX tweet[67] with video of the crash landing and the text, "Close, but no cigar. This time." In space terms even hitting the barge was an incredible success. Since the public "failure" SpaceX has gone on to successfully land rockets and reuse them for ensuing launches, all at a tenth of the average launch cost. A new era of space travel has emerged because someone followed a dream and knew that failure was in fact a cutting edge achievement.

My last failure (I've had a few) I could see coming a mile away. I didn't want to acknowledge the reality that was staring me in the

[66] About SpaceX, SpaceX, accessed January 5th, 2015, http://www.spacex.com/about/

[67] SpaceX (@SpaceX), "Close, but no cigar. This time.," Twitter, January 16, 2015, 9:50 a.m., https://twitter.com/SpaceX/status/556131313905070081

face—or should I say, five people were staring at me. Three were my family and two came late. I didn't know it at the time, but this was the final Sunday service for my church plant I had started seven years prior. We went out with a whimper. If you are a pastor, imagine the feeling if six people showed up to your church service. You might quit on the spot. As a church planter and entrepreneur I've gone through failure many times before but I still wasn't fully prepared for the loss. I was stuck with a deeply ingrained piece of church culture that connected numbers and success. I couldn't help but see the failure defined in the size of the service.

The way most deal with the prospect of failure in the face of trying something new is to ignore or mitigate it. If we can avoid failure, or work out a plan to hold it at bay, we will. It follows the false assumption that with enough of ourselves, be it gifts, skills, and most of all hard work, we'll make it. But that's a calling again more in a world where we need *deeper* with what we already have. Starting or being a part of new things means you're going to fail more than the alternative—staying safe and doing nothing. Ask yourself this, if you knew your dream in community could come true, but it came with a cost, would you take it? What's your limit? What if the cost was 25% of your congregation or group? What if it was 25% of your budget or 25% of your income? Would you give up 25% of what you have now for 3% growth every year? Or is the prospect of failure too great? What if we changed our outlook of failure and made an acceptable outcome?

Here's the reality that even SpaceX confirms: even the best plans succumb to defeat. When I started my first church plant I was a recent economics major and ran my own business. Strategic planning was my thing. Plans, strategies, budgets, I could create them over a coffee. I had an array of impressive models and tactics to go with them. I had the plans man! Then something ruined the plans—people. It didn't take long to realize my great plans weren't so great. Great plans can't replace the foremost step of turning our dreams real: building relationships with people who will join the fray. The best plans fall through when you don't put relationships at the forefront of your activity.

When you start to turn ideas real be it in business, life change, or living out your kingdom calling, branching outside of the box takes courage and leaves you in an empty place because you're going where few others will. If your idea fails, I hope it happens in the midst of a loving community and that you lean into the calamity so the next stage of change can present itself. Unfortunately, sometimes risk takers are left outside to freeze. If that's your situation, send me an email and I'll lament with you. But when all else fails, cling to this: no matter what, God is in your midst. In the desert, ask God to reveal signs to help make sense of your triumphs and failure.

Pioneer by Signposts

Oprah Winfrey has a movement of followers chasing wellness, but her popularity is predicated on the *cost* to participate. It's negligible. Church community is significantly different because it's supposed to be countercultural. Where consumerism says you deserve what you desire, Christ said deny yourself for the sake of the kingdom.

Because the cost to follow Jesus is great, often Christians pray hard for visible signs or audible calls from God to confirm the dreams and ideas they have. More often that signal doesn't come. If I had waited for a demonstrable "voice from God" to confirm my calling, I'd still be waiting (not that they haven't happened to me). Search Amazon for titles on "hearing the voice of God" and a plethora of titles will emerge. We long for the audible voice of God to confirm our calling and direction. But what if God has already given us the answers and pieces needed to start? Perhaps our prayers should be less about whether or not we should *start* down an unknown path, and instead requests for *confirming* signposts as we go.

I was lucky to encounter like-minded individuals early on in my church planting start. The community confirmed the idea and legitimized what was a crazy idea on its own. I also had signposts that pointed out areas of growth. Being nondenominational meant I was largely alone. Loneliness is both a reality and a threat for pioneers. Compounding this loneliness was the fact that I also ran a number of my own businesses, which means I work from home. There were days where I didn't even *see* another human. This is an extreme that's not healthy, and something I've had to note and remedy. You have to be okay with being alone when trying something new. On the other hand, there's a level of spiritual formation and health that must be cultivated to withstand the loneliness. You have to be okay operating without much affirmation from other people and without the accolades of a job well done.

A word of warning: As you progress through the loneliness and obscurity that accompanies change, remember toughening it out isn't a healthy strategy. Do what you must to enact rhythms that invite the voices of mentors, spiritual directors, counselors, and peers to whom you can vent and grow. It's pre-emptive work to stay safe in the face of constant failure. These people also act as guides and signposts along the way to help our ideas and communities grow.

Pioneering, exploring, and stretching out into the unknown are innate human qualities. When we risk, we face our fears and enter the fog in hopes that once it lifts beauty—not the edge of a cliff—will be revealed. Being fearless isn't a prerequisite to embark on new adventures. Fear necessitates courage and courage is necessary when trying new things. Good planning will waylay some concerns, but here's my truth. Living out a dream for better while turning ideas real may be lonely and fraught with failure. Confront your fears by creating your own "liturgy" that points to a reliance on God at every step along the way. God's hope can triumph at every stage, we just need to be ready.

Chapter 26

Never Give Up

"The harvest is plentiful but the workers are few."
- Matthew 9:37 (NIV)

*E*arlier I told the story about the end of my first church plant. I promised to share the second part. Months after my church plant of seven years ended a new opportunity emerged, seemingly out of nowhere. During the short transition I had a distinct sense something else was coming. I had no obvious opportunities in front of me but I just had an unknown peace with my situation. Then, two days before Christmas the message came. But first, let's rewind a couple of years for context.

My friend Connie (whom I introduced earlier) and I used to meet to pray for a community that would include the religious nones, particular those in the urban demographic. The idea kept coming up but it never amounted to anything more than a prayer night or two. I had once suggested that it sounded like a church planting opportunity. She had little interest in that idea. So we continued meeting sporadically to pray and muse about what could be done with our vague idea. Then, a few weeks after the final service where six people showed, and two days before Christmas, I received a message. "What do you think about doing an event?"

An event was the last thing I was interested in doing. Sure, I was looking for something new, but launching new expression just for the sake of being cool, like an evening service, wasn't my idea of responding with depth to God's mission. I had no interest in new wine in old wineskins. Nonetheless, I thought about a response and sent this two days later, knowing full well what the reply had been in the past, "I'm not interested in an event. But I'll do a church plant." Her response caught me off guard, "I'm in!" I don't know what changed other than God's timing was right. Two months after that conversation Cypher Church[68] launched its first service. The rest is history in the making.

Now, in order to understand what I'm about to say next you need to know something about me. I'm not easily impressed. I see beauty and power in simple things, but I am slow to get overly excited. Having said that, the opening night for Cypher Church was *incredible* and everything we could have hoped for in an event. The service itself worked. Cyphers can only be planned to a certain extent, the rest relies on the invitation to artists, dancers, musicians, and rappers to bring their gift to the circle. On launch night our cypher was hot! All sorts of people were dancing, singing, rapping, an electric launch to say the least. But that wasn't the only success. The transformations we saw that evening, some that still unravel today, blew me away. People were experiencing healings, spiritual transformations, Christians who thought they were done with faith were starting to see a place they could call home, and then there was the man with a heavy heart. He showed up at our service walk-

---

[68] Check us out at http://cypherchurch.com for an idea of what our events look like. Bear in mind, it's not something you can replicate in your context. What gave us early success was existing relationship in the music/dance community, not because the events themselves were incredible. They are attractive, but that's not the primary reason why people come.

ing in right off the street. He saw some people his age walking into the building and randomly decided to follow. Where he was going, he would later confess, was unknown. All he knew was he planned to walk until he couldn't walk anymore, and there he would kill himself. Instead, he arrived near the end of our event during a raw spoken word piece. The words from the poet, along with his situation, brought him to his knees. He was confronted by his burdens and sought a release. With his head in his hands he muttered to someone, "I need to confess." Four of us found a quiet room, and once we sat down two things happened: he received spiritual renewal asking Jesus to heal him, and he confessed to some major crimes. That evening, amidst all of the energy, the angels rejoiced as this man entered the kingdom, while we looked on in bewilderment as he left our event in the back of the police truck I had called.

Since that day Cypher Church has been a curious experiment that continues to surprise us. Random people keep coming off the street to join our events. Every gathering features new people we've never seen, and people who've never heard the gospel story before. All of this happened not because of my ability (or even from the co-pastor), but through the faithful leap to respond with a "yes" to our moment of opportunity. We are showing up to a field where the harvest is waiting.

Case Study: From the Institution

My friend D graduated seminary a year ahead of me yet we had classes together during the two years we overlapped. D is a gifted leader and accepted a role as a lead pastor right out of school (which is rare). One thing about D is he's constantly responding to the mission God has laid out for him and his family. He had little interest merely operating as a traditional shepherd pastor maintaining an

English congregation of an ethnic church. Instead, he embarked on a journey to compel a congregation of 150 people to discover their calling to God's kingdom unfolding in the neighborhood. To do so would mean radically changing the paradigm of the very conventional, yet young, congregation. It would require considerable discipleship to turn consumers into participants, it would take a considerable time investment, and it would risk alienating those who just wanted a quiet Sunday service to attend. After seeking input, D put together a plan and started. It wasn't long before resistance arrived.

In year one 25% of the congregation left for a less challenging Christian experience. With them went some security as well (namely in tithes). However, there were gains. A new generation of leaders started to emerge, and they were getting excited about their work in the community. Neighborhoods were also noticing the church at work in the community.

It took just under three years (I think this is fast by the way) before a new rhythm for the church emerged. Could you stomach losing a quarter of your budget and people for the sake of the gospel? Most of us can't. They took a risk and were rewarded. Three years later the people didn't look much different, and the services were about the same as well. But the activities in the church changed. Because the congregation saw their role as the hands and feet of Jesus in the neighborhood, the number of transformations was beyond their expectations. New favor from the city due to the trust they developed through relationships, people coming to faith, healings in their midst, new responsibility to improve communities beyond the church, affordable housing, medical clinics, after school classes, community youth programs, all of these expressions found a natural fit within the ethos of a church that dared to say yes to new opportunities in their midst. By shifting their thinking from what the church program could do for the neighborhood, they incarnated presence and demonstrated the gospel by loving the neighborhood first. As the new rhythm for D's church interconnected with the heartbeat of the neighborhood, it now had a heartbeat for Jesus.

How you receive your calling, how you capture your dream for better, how you live out your ideas to turn your world into a better place, it's all unique to your place and space. But what remains unchanged is the result of those things. The fruit of your attempt and faithfulness to your calling is wrapped up in the stories of the people you encounter. Stories of transformations, healings, reconciliations and restoration. Stories of our participating in the unfolding kingdom hope to right wrongs in our neighborhood, city, and world. All of this represents the result—the reward—for our work. Cypher Church "only" has 40-75 people at any given event. It's not a mega church by any means. But for the small resource we have, and for the small yet growing cadre of dreamers who are calling it home, I can't think of a better place or community to call "church."

We all want some tangible result from our work to validate the process and our efforts. I would like to say that the reward for your faithful service will be a movement that springs new church plants, transformations of entire neighborhoods, or the discipleship of multitudes of people. I hope it does, but maybe it won't. Yet that doesn't mean failure. Our reward may simply be wrapped up in the stories that we're a part of as we open our eyes and heart to the kingdom at work in our midst. And through all of this work, one day we will receive the words, "Well done, good and faithful servant. Well done!"

⁹"As the Father has loved me, so have I loved you. Now remain in my love. ¹⁰If you keep my commands, you will remain in my love, just as I have kept my Father's commands and remain in his love. ¹¹I have told you this so that my joy may be in you and that your joy may be complete. ¹²My command is this: Love each other as I have loved you. ¹³Greater love has no one than this: to lay down one's life for one's friends. ¹⁴You are my friends if you do what I command. ¹⁵I no longer call you servants, because a servant does not know his master's business. Instead, I have called you friends, for everything that I learned from my Father I have made known to you. ¹⁶You did not choose me, but I chose you and appointed you so that you might go and bear fruit—fruit that will last—and so that whatever you ask in my name the Father will give you. ¹⁷This is my command: Love each other. - (John 15:9-17, NIV)

Chapter 27

The End With No Return

"Let us arise, then, at last,
For the Scripture stirs us up, saying,
"Now is the hour for us to rise from sleep." (Romans 13:11)"
- Prologue from Saint Benedict's Rule for Monasteries

I prefer the book ending over the film in Tolkien's *Return of the King*. If you've read the classic you would remember the fight for Middle Earth does not leave the Shire unscathed. The hobbits return to find their home in shambles, where yet another battle must be won. The film, on the other hand, pictures Frodo, Sam, Merri, and Pippin trudging into the picturesque Shire exhausted and changed following their harrowing adventure. They have joyful reunions with oblivious friends and family blissfully unaware of the calamity that broached their doorstep. For the heroes, their return wasn't entirely a happy ending. While they were transformed by adventure, their ordinary world had remained unchanged. You could tell that although the heroes were relieved to return to their old routines, they lamented over the sheltered hobbits who would never know about the world that twisted around them.

I remember attending a lecture by missiologist Darrel Guder. He was speaking at an old Presbyterian church, and by old I don't mean the building: I was the youngest person by 30 years. As Guder unpacked the ideas for a missional posture—living God's hope of restoration in the mission field here at home—the congregation was struggling to link the ideas to practical applications. One man stood to ask a question that reflected the shared lament in the church.

"We've done all that we can to raise our now adult children in the ways they should go. We brought them to church and taught them our values. Yet today they no longer come to church nor value the same things we did. Where did we go wrong? We've tried everything."

This man's concern reveals a dominant narrative in the contemporary church, namely, mission is the way the church can return to a past era. I understand where he's coming from and his hope. To him, successful mission is recapturing his picture of church and culture. A time when churches fought to keep shops closed on Sundays so families could have time to eat and spend time together. That's not to say everything from his past lacks value. But some churches are dying because they are unable to accept change in a new culture for the sake of building the local church body. Culture doesn't go back in time. This man wanted a revival of sorts, but to what? To his *own* lost culture. It's no wonder his kids don't come to church anymore. They don't want to inherit dad's past life. They want to create their own future. The next generation wants to be inspired *towards* something that works for their lives today. They don't want to be called back to reclaim someone else's heritage that only worked for certain people.

Christians spend a lot of resources trying to return the church to the heyday of yesteryear. Recapturing past prestige consumes their thinking and effort. These activities in turn produce a church identity that lacks a suitable direction for moving forward and surviving cultural shifts. We can't reclaim a particular golden age where the church was the center of attention, where we could wait for the world to ask the church for answers to life's questions. I think the loss is a good thing. The church with power became complacent with its mission. Inherited privilege contributed to decades (perhaps centuries) of atrophy and a dwindling competency on how to bear the character of Jesus as a witness to the world. We must discover what change needs to be implemented today, because if we continue to fail we will see the further disintegration of the church in the West. Rather than taking a road back into the desert, we need to be more like Chuck Nolan at the crossroads in *Castaway*. We must choose the next direction and *go* with new ideas that spring new hope for a church to thrive tomorrow. We are in a moment of profound opportunity. The church must re-discover the subversive gospel and become co-leaders in a "spiritual but not religious" generation. Nones and dones long for the hidden gift of God's story that features the fullness of justice, beauty, restoration, purpose, hope, and most of all a love that knows no bounds. This is the dream of the missionary God who pursues restoration for all creation.

God Chases After You

From the Garden to the Flood; the Desert to the Exodus; the Promised Land through the Priests; the Priests through the Kings; the Kings through the Prophets; the Prophets to the Exile; the Exile to the Son; the Son to the Cross; the Cross to the Grave; the Grave to the Resurrection; the Resurrection to Ascension; the Ascension to Pentecost; the Spirit to the Church. Throughout history God chases after you with an invitation to participate in the unwavering dream to put the world to rights. It's a grand invitation that cherishes the value of your dreams and ideas too, beckoning you to live out your dream for better.

That's not to say our road isn't fraught with peril. Every major story in the Bible saw apparent defeat and sometimes death. The death of Jesus was an initial defeat for the disciples. In their loss they could not see how the cross paved the way for the forgiveness of sins that ultimately robs evil of its power. They could not see the greatest moment in human history was about to unravel in resurrection. They were unaware God's kingdom was about to be inaugurated and the ultimate sin—death—would be conquered once and for all. They could not expect that the resurrection was in their midst and a total triumph was their new story. This new story is the same task given to the church—to you and me—to act as critical pieces previewing God's dream here and now. As we have graciously received we must graciously respond in faithfulness to the calling to a harvest. Jesus told his disciples, "Go! Live out my dream in the four corners of the earth. Go! Live out my commands to love justice, love beauty, love my dream of hope, and love to love and be loved." And to what end? A return to the Garden? Eternity spent in heaven up in the clouds? No. That Garden was abandoned at the beginning of time and won't be reclaimed. Going back is never the option—something better is in play. God's story ends with the collision of two worlds: New Heaven and New Earth brought together forever.

Fin

When I started this book I asked you to picture the best dream possible and work towards bringing a piece of that idea to life. We all have ideas, dreams, and aspirations, but ideas by themselves are worth little. You can't turn back and reclaim the way the world once was. You must *do* something with your dream. Responding to God's invitation to live out your gifts and abilities is what counts. It's the embodied activity that includes the *one* act, the *one* moment, the *one* choice you make to live out the fullness of God's plan for you and your community. Of course, this road contains changes big and small, and the cost of change could be steep. It may lead to pain, heartache, and even death. But in death and pain there is new life. Deep down the pursuit of living out our callings is better than the discomfort. We all want to matter in a story that includes our ideas for better. Which is exactly what the world needs: your dreams and ideas that reveal God's picture for the best life has to offer.

The time to live out the fullness of God's calling is now. Will you say "yes" to turn your dreams for better real? Within your journey are the pieces that help propel you and your community forward to ultimately survive and *thrive* in our neighborhoods and cities today and beyond. Respond now to your human longings. Live out your dreams to join God's extraordinary story that ends with the final triumph of good over evil. Enjoy the journey.

A prayer for journeys.

"Stand at the crossroads and look;
ask for the ancient paths,
ask where the good way is, and walk in it,
and you will find rest for your souls."
- Jeremiah 6:16 (NIV)

Bibliography

Bibby, Reginald. *Resilient Gods. Being Pro-religious, Low Religious, or No Religious in Canada.* Vancouver: UBC Press, 2017.

Bosch, David. *Transforming Mission: paradigm Shifts in Theology of Mission.* 20th ed. Maryknoll: Orbis Books, 2011.

Brafman, Ori, and Judah Pollack. *The Chaos Imperative. How chance and disruption Increase Innovation, Effectiveness, and Success.* New York. Crown Business, 2013

Brafman, Ori, and Rod A. Beckstrom. *The Starfish and the Spider.* New York: Penguin Group, 2007.

Catmull, Edwin. *Creativity Inc. Overcoming The Unseen Forces That Stand In The Way Of True Inspiration.* Toronto: Random House Canada, 2014.

Christensen, Clayton M. *The Innovators Dilemma. When new technologies cause great firms to fail.* Boston: HBRP, 2013.

Cleveland, Christena. *Disunity in Christ. Uncovering the hidden forces that keep us apart.* Downers Grove: InterVarsity Press, 2013.

Emerson, Michael O, and Christian Smith. *Divided by Faith. Evangelical religion and the problem of race in America.* New York: Oxford University Press, 2000.

Feldmann, Derrick. *Social Movements for Good. How Companies and Causes Create Viral Change.* Hoboken: John Wiley and Sons, 2016.

Frost, Michael. *Incarnate: The Body of Christ in an Age of Disengagement.* Downers Grove: Intervarsity Press, 2014.

Garrison, David. *Church Planting Movements. How God is Redeeming a Lost World.* Banglore: WIGTake Resources, 2004.

Guder, Darrell L. *Missional Church: A Vision for the Sending of the Church in North America.* Grand Rapids: Eerdmans, 1998.

Guder, Darrell L. *The Incarnation and the Church's Witness.* Harrisburg: Trinity Press International, 1999.

Hirsch, Alan, and Tim Catchim. *The Permanent Revolution. The Apostolic Imagination and Practice for the 21st Century Church.* San Francisco: Josey-Bass, 2012.

Johnston, Hank. *What is a Social Movement?* Cambridge: Polity Press, 2014.

Jones, Robert P. *The End of White Christian America.* New York: Simon-Schuster, 2016.

Malherbe, Abraham J. *Social Aspects of Early Christianity.* Baton Rouge: Louisiana State University Press, 2007.

Marti, Gerardo, and Gladys Ganiel. *The Deconstructed Church. Understanding Emerging Christianity.* New York: Oxford University Press, 2014.

Moreau, Scott. *Contextualization in World Missions: Mapping and Assessing Evangelical models*. Grand Rapids: Kregel, 2012.

Newbigin, Leslie. *The Open Secret. An Introduction to the Theology of Mission*. Rev ed. Grand Rapid: Eerdmans, 1995.

Newbigin, Leslie. *Gospel in a Pluralist Society*. Grand Rapid: Eerdmans, 1989.

Popovic, Srdja, and Matthew Miller. *Blueprint for Revolution: How to Use Rice Pudding, Lego Men, and Other Nonviolent Techniques to Galvanize Communities, Overthrow Dictators, or Simply Change the World*. New York: Spiegel & Grau, 2015.

Roberts, Bob Jr. *Glocalization: How Followers of Jesus Engage a Flat World*. Grand Rapids: Zondervan, 2007.

Roxburgh, Alan J. *The Missionary Congregation, Leadership, and Liminality*. Harrisburg: Trinity Press International, 1997.

Stark, Rodney. *Cities of God. The Real Story of how Christianity Became an Urban Moment and Conquered Rome*. New York: HarperCollins, 2006.

Stark, Rodney. *The Triumph of Christianity. How the Jesus Movement Became the World's Largest Religion*. New York: HarperOne, 2011.

Stott, John, and Christopher J.H. Writer. *Christian Mission in the Modern World*. (Updated and expanded). Downers Grove: InterVarsity Books, 2015.

Tickle, Phyllis. *The Great Emergence. How Christianity is Changing and Why*. Grand Rapids: Baker Books, 2008.

Thiessen, Joel. *The Meaning of Sunday: The Practice of Belief in a Secular Age*. Montreal-Kingston: McGill-Queen's University Press, 2015.

Wright, N.T. *The Day the Revolution Began: Reconsidering the Meaning of Jesus's Crucifixion*. San Francisco: Harper One, 2016

Wright, N.T. *Surprised by Hope: Rethinking Heaven, the Resurrection, and the Mission of the Church*. New York: Harper Collins, 2008.

Author's Note

Most writers will tell you writing is a lonely enterprise. This book took three years to put together writing, rewriting, submitting, editing, until the coherent form you have before you came to be. My first thank you is to you, the reader, for embarking on this book adventure. It's risky to pick up an indie book from an unknown author. I hope you found some important ideas on how to turn your dreams real. Could I ask for two things? One, would you pass this book along or recommend it to a friend? It helps get the word out. Second, let's connect. Share your story about how you're living out new ideas in your world. I'd love to hear about them and I promise to reply. Find me online **@rohadi** on Twitter or **www.rohadi.com**

A number of people helped guide this book into its final form. The first readers who graciously spent time. They include: Jean Dowson, Cindy Nagassar, Rob Scott, Preston Pouteaux, and Tim Schultz. Jared Siebert, David Ruis, and Tim Schultz added their voice in the acknowledgments. J.R. Woodward went above and beyond by writing the foreword and providing feedback. Kevin Miller provided developmental editing while Amanda Phifer copyedited. Alyssa Minor aided with proofing. The book cover was a team effort with Riley Rossmo and Ryan Lee. V4Victory completed the book layout. Thank you to all.

Made in the USA
Las Vegas, NV
27 September 2021

31241876R00125